MICROTONAL HEALING

Healing occurs in a sacred, microtonal space

that can be likened to Great Mystery.

The voice is the natural instrument

to directly access that space with healing energy.

LINDA L. NIELSEN, PH.D.

microtonal healing

•

SPIRIT
OF
THE
HEALING
VOICE

DeVorss Publications
Camarillo, California

ISBN: 0875167942
Library of Congress Control Number: 2003113779
First Printing, 2004

DeVorss & Company, Publisher
P.O. Box 1389
Camarillo CA 93011-1389
w w w . d e v o r s s . c o m
Printed in the United States of America

For my parents
Henry Nielsen
and
Evelyn Rodrigues Nielsen
who encouraged
my Spirit to soar.

CONTENTS

ACKNOWLEDGMENTS

Thank you to those who have given their time and support to me in so many ways during the creation of this book.

To Dan Moonhawk Alford who encouraged my initial microtonal healing research efforts along with Margaret Mackenzie, Karolyn van Putten, Fariba Bogzaran, Patricia Lynn Mann, Sophia Roberts, and Norma Zamit.

To Phillip Scott, Lynn Sydney, and Sanaya Roman for bringing another dimension of support through the love and light of Great Spirit and Divine Consciousness.

To my friend and teacher, Silvia Nakkach, I offer praises of thanks for her kind guidance in teaching me to find my microtonal voice. She enabled an opening through which I began to perceive the world through a microtonal lens; I am eternally grateful.

A special thank you is extended to Dr. Valerie Hunt who so graciously gave her time and energy to read and comment on the manuscript draft. I am grateful for her enthusiasm and permission to quote from her book *Infinite Mind*.

To Heidi Rosenberg, Michael Melchior, Cody Melchior, Richie McKenzie, Scott McKenzie, Wendy Mckenzie Ryan, Margaret Wilkenfeld, Dave Nielsen, Rick Nielsen, and Rod Nielsen, thank you for your love and belief in me.

To Patricia Hartigan Bloom, Ann Cory, Cisco Emas, Sue Anne Torres, Alyce Linscott, Darlene deManincor, Cindy Olney, Maxine Olney, Paul Rosenberg, Jules Davis, Priscilla Stuckey, Julie Spencer, Julie Dillman, Linda Patrick, and Maureen Stapler-Crowell for your enthusiasm and encouragement.

Thank you to Kim Robinson, my editor at DeVorss & Company, for her support and vision in refining my work.

To Gary Peattie, thank you for bringing this book to light.

INTRODUCTION

Nighttime unfolds dreams rich with inspiration and creative ideas. Upon awakening, the artist clings to an
image. The poet senses a rhythm that lends itself to poetry.
The composer hears music stirring beneath wakefulness. And
so it is for me. Teachings are given to me in my dreams. This
book was called forth by a dream I had at a time when I was
researching the healing voice. In this dream, I was handed a
book entitled *Microtonal Healing*, which I was to write.
Upon awakening, I brought with me the title, an image of a
band of colors, and an awareness that the book held information to quench my curiosity about how the voice heals. The
process of writing the book did just that and now I pass the
information on to you.

Healing in the context of a microtonal theoretical framework is at the heart of this book. It contributes to the body of
knowledge currently available on the healing voice by intro-
ducing microtonal concepts to explain and clarify processes
of healing. Microtonal healing is an evolving theory that orig-
inated in my dream and grew out of my own microtonal
singing practice and observations of life processes. It rests on
the premise that healing occurs in a microtonal space in
which the potential for transformation to well-being exists.
This has become the thesis of my work.

The healing voice is a subject that has been discussed primarily within the context of musical harmonics, and overtone chanting has often been the vocal method explored. I came to see that harmonic theory does not always explain the function of the healing voice, and musical theory presented in sound healing literature has not addressed the healing process that is initiated by vocal practices.

Microtonal healing with the voice is a process that involves an integration of vocal healing practices. Dissertation research provided an opportunity for me to gather participant responses to two vocal practices related to well-being. One group of volunteers reported their experiences in response to overtone chanting while a second group responded to the practice of microtonal singing over a four-week period. Although overtone chanting has been widely discussed within the sound healing community as a whole, the practice has not been systematically investigated and documented from the experiential perspective as it is presented in my dissertation "In Search of Healing Voices" (Nielsen 2000). Having responses to two practices established a basis for comparison. My dissertation was also a vehicle with which to formally introduce microtonal healing concepts initiated in my dream. This book investigates those concepts in depth.

Microtonal Healing is designed to take the reader into an exploration of the vocal healing experience. Along with this is a rationale for understanding the healing voice. It informs newcomers as well as those familiar with concepts of holistic health and energy medicine.

Section 1, Cornerstones of the Healing Voice, places the creative power of the voice in a historical context and addresses how the voice functions as an instrument of healing.

Section 2, Microtonal Singing, introduces microtonal singing as a format for developing and nurturing cognitive awareness of the micromovements involved in maintaining a state of balance and well-being. It begins with honoring your voice and creating a sacred space in which to sing. Microtonal singing is based on raga form music. The music of North India is therefore presented to provide an understanding of the nature of microtones and their place in the musical structure. Practical applications are then offered to develop mindfulness of microtonal healing processes by way of the microtonal singing voice.

Microtonal concepts are presented in Section 3. An in-depth discussion of the space between is enlivened with exercises to comprehend that space from an experiential perspective. The microtonal space gives way to the flow of life, which invites observation of the natural environment through a microtonal lens. Taking microtonal singing on a walk with nature allows the voice to unfold in a natural splendor.

Having an array of vocal techniques available and understanding the characteristics of each practice is essential to using them for optimum benefit. Section 4, Weaving Vocal Tapestries, offers some guidelines as to which practices most directly access emotional content, which practices soothe and relieve emotional buildup, and which practices provide a means of achieving focus or a transcendent state.

Section 5, Final Notes, offers summary thoughts on microtonal healing as a therapeutic process of following the voice of the heart. It invites the reader to explore the dream image that initiated this book and provides personal background that prepared the way for me to unravel the content of my dream and translate it into written form.

The goal of *Microtonal Healing* is to demonstrate that the voice is vibrational medicine. The voice complements natural healing processes and, as such, it is the most vital and noninvasive tool for maintaining and restoring well-being. I encourage everyone who can speak to tune body, mind and spirit daily with vocal practices for health.

With the gift of listening comes the gift of healing.

— Catherine de Hueck

1
CORNERSTONES OF
THE HEALING VOICE

VOICES OF CREATION

The sacredness of the voice has long been recognized in the form of prayerful utterances. Creation stories and healing practices of indigenous peoples reflect beliefs that embrace the creative and healing power of sound, primarily in the form of song and by way of breath instruments. Song and word and breath convey the power of creator as transformer and healer. Life forms are called into being with word, naming, humming, or singing. These sounds emanate from the voice and flow from the breath of Spirit. In the Hopi tradition, for example, Spider Woman mixed earth with her saliva to mold two beings. Singing the Creation Song, she gave them life. They undertook the duties of keeping the world in order by tuning everything to the sound of the Creator. Spider Woman then molded all the birds and animals and sang over them to give them life. So, too, with the first people of the Hopi. They were given life when Spider Woman sang the Song of Creation over their forms (Waters 1977).

Among the Amazonian Wakuénai (Hill 1993), the creative force emanates from a sacred flute. As an instrument of the breath, a flute is indicative of breathing life into inanimate objects. The flute is held as sacred and symbolizes the multivocal creative powers of Kuwái, the primordial being who opened up the world and sang all bird, fish, and animal species into being. In mythology of the Bororo in central Brazil, the hero restores life to people who had drowned in a flood by chanting invocations along with drumming (Levi-Strauss 1975).

Healing with song and music continues to be a common practice used by traditional healers around the world. Among the Montagnais, the native people of northern Quebec and Labrador, the principal method of healing is song (Peat 1994). For them, it is the song that heals, the process of singing that heals. The spirit of the song contains the animating and healing power. The Hopi sing to create change and restore well-being. They recognize that the healing power of music will help a sick child to heal (Waters 1977). This is also the way of the Navajo who sing the Snake Song to effect renewal, regeneration, and restoration of health (Witherspoon 1997).

In North India, the ghost healers of Hindu tradition invoke the compassion of disease-causing spirits using song and silent mantras (Cook 1997). A Peruvian Ayahuasca shaman uses icaros, tunes without words, which are played on a harmonica. Songs are sung in the ancient Inca language, Quechua, to strengthen the Ayahuasca and to help people heal at the deepest levels (Ibid.). The concept of health and well-being in these age-old traditions is one that appears to embrace an integrative balance of body-mind-emotions-spirit.

The use of song and chant in ancient healing rituals can be traced to teachings of antiquity found in Europe, Asia, China, Tibet, and the Americas. Systems of sound healing were also used in Egypt (Keyes 1990; Tame 1984; Gerber 1988). The ankh, a cross with an elongated loop at the top, is referred to as the key of life. More than a symbol of healing and enduring life, the ankh was used in Egyptian rituals to amplify the healing vibrations of sound. In ancient Greece, Pythagoras used music and voice as medicine to restore harmony and well-being in a person. This healing influence of sound had a resurgence in Greece during the Renaissance but it did not endure beyond that era (Rudhyar 1982).

Over the past forty or fifty years, some vocal sound healers in the United States have begun their healing practices after experiencing the need to express tones that suddenly rose up from within. For example, Laurel Elizabeth Keyes (1990) discovered her healing voice in 1959 when she felt compelled to sound a tone. After several attempts to ignore the urge to sound, the inner tone won out and the sound rose up from the depths of her being. Noticing how exhilarated and alive she felt after toning, she developed toning into a spiritual practice. Toning became her connection to God. Through continued exploration of her voice, she learned to direct her tones into different parts of her body for healing. She taught others to tone and presented her research on the ancient practice of toning at workshops and conferences.

Today, a community of vocal sound healers is coming into being in the United States. It is comprised of a group of people, primarily women, who have found meaning in vocal healing practices. My research indicates that sound healers are often drawn to vocal healing through dramatic personal experiences that were turning points in their lives, and meaning arises from within each sound healer's story. The meaning is personal, yet there is a common bonding around meaning, a basic agreement with regard to the role of the voice in creation, transformation, and healing.

Many vocal sound healers discovered their healing sounds independently. In the absence of an established community of vocal healing practitioners to draw on, they had no alternative but to explore the effects of vocal practices in isolation. The use of the voice in the healing process unfolded for them individually. Methods and applications of vocal practices developed based on their own vocal healing experiences and perceptions of energy. It is common for a variety of vocal practices to come together in their work, including body sounds, melodic sounds, overtone chanting, and vocables (syllabic sounds without meaning).

The application of vocal techniques and practices is unique to the individual sound healer. As an example, many sound healers use a form of vocable sounding in their therapeutic work. For some, vocables are a method of emotional expression. For others, vocables come forth from Universal Mind and are integral to the beauty of the healing sounds they sing and chant. In addition to using their own voices to restore balance and well-being for their clients, the sound health practitioners with whom I have spoken and worked serve as guides in helping others find their own vocal healing sounds. They are grounded in compassion and transmit an awareness of the spiritual aspect of their healing work. Vocal sound healing is their life's work.

The use of the voice as a complementary healing modality is a new and expanding field that is supported by ancient traditions as well as by the new physics. Nevertheless, study of the healing voice is primarily experiential. The mystery around vocal healing processes needs to fall away if it is to be accepted as a viable discipline in the healing arts. Understanding the healing process by way of microtonal singing permits conscious exploration of that mystery. Microtonal concepts reveal healing processes in general as well as the need to draw on the wisdom and findings of other disciplines, particularly in the physical sciences.

FOUNDATIONS OF SOUND HEALING AND THE HEALING VOICE

The principles on which healing with sound rest are basic concepts of energy or vibrational medicine. Energy medicine is not new and its principles are not complex. It is being called forth from ancient traditions around the world, particularly in practices such as Yoga and acupuncture found in eastern cultures. To understand vocal sound healing as a form of energy work requires approaching the topic from a cultural paradigm or worldview that embraces concepts of vibration, frequency, and resonance. The cultural paradigm to which I refer is that of sound healers.

A cultural paradigm is the way in which reality is perceived by a group of people. It is psychically cohesive, providing a sense of order and meaning within which to live and to perceive life. For sound healers, psychic cohesiveness, order, and meaning stem from what they perceive as the vibrational nature of the universe and spiritual values that acknowledge a oneness of life. The language of sound healers is descriptive of a worldview that reflects a belief in systems of energy beyond those that can be perceived by the physical senses of most humans. Theirs is a language of concepts that acknowledge not only the visible physical world but also invisible worlds. We live in both.

15

A HOLISTIC APPROACH
TO HEALING

The paradigm of sound healers and others who work in energy medicine is said to be holistic. A holistic approach to healing is one that acknowledges a synergy or union between the body-mind-emotions-spirit of a person. When these aspects of well-being are in harmonic balance, a person is said to be in a state of health. Body-mind-emotions-spirit are best perceived as a continuum of energy in which the body merges with the energy field. Health is seen as a state of wholeness, and healing is the process of making whole.

The concept of healing in holistic terms is one that has been gaining recognition in recent years among the general population in the United States. As a result, the medical community has opened its doors to some complementary health practices, including energy medicine. Vocal sound healing is a form of energy medicine that accesses every aspect of being, yet it is scarcely acknowledged in clinical settings. Healing is a natural process because the tendency of the body is to return to a point of healthful balance (Pert 1999; Weil 1995). The voice complements natural healing processes and, as such, is a vital and noninvasive tool for maintaining and restoring that balance.

VIBRATION, FREQUENCY AND RESONANCE

A basic assumption of sound healers is that the composition of the body and of the entire universe is not only sound but music. Every organ in the body vibrates at a different frequency, and according to Andrews (1966) and Lynes (1999), every chemical in the body emanates a unique sound. Every object and being in the universe vibrates with a specific frequency based on its structure and the particular vibrational rate of the atoms that compose it (Andrews 1966; Wolf 1992). The vibrational frequency for each individual is therefore unique, and because of the chemical reactions that occur within the body throughout the day, the frequency of the physical body is in a constant state of flux. Our music changes with the vibrational fluctuations.

As musical beings, we require regular tuning, or attunement, terms that refer to the process of restoring resonance and well-being using forms of energy work. Some methods used by sound healers in their attunement work are music, tuning forks, and vocal sounds such as singing, chanting, and toning. Rhythmic drumming is also employed in healing with sound. Drums have tones that affect mental well-being and specific parts of the body according to Wolf (1992) and Diallo and Hall (1989). Other forms of vibrational medicine such as Reiki, acupuncture, acupressure, and color therapy are also used to perform attunements.

CHAKRAS, AURA
AND THE ENERGY FIELD

As musical beings, each person is an individual composition that is unlike any other person. The composition is made up of subtle sounds that are beyond physical auditory perception. Among sound healers, the word "subtle" is used in conjunction with the vibrational energy of the aura, chakras or energy centers, and the life force that flows through our bodies and the energy field. Life force is commonly described as vital energy, a dynamic invisible energy that flows through our being. This life force is referred to as "Chi" in Chinese traditions, "Prana" in India, and "Qi" in Japan. Subtle is descriptive of energy so refined it is imperceptible to our five senses, although it is visible or otherwise perceptible to some people. Subtle energy refers to the finer vibrations of higher frequencies that inhabit the invisible world.

Chakra is a Sanskrit word that means "wheel." As centers of subtle energy, chakras are spiritual openings through which the life force flows. Chakras are perceived as colorful whirling disks about one and a half inches in diameter, the size of a silver dollar. There are seven primary chakras located along the nerve network of the spine and at the top of the head of the human body (Hills 1979; Hunt 1996; Schwarz 1980; Twitchell 1982). Chakras are also called astral lotuses (Yogananda 1990) and are sometimes illustrated as open flowers.

The aura consists of subtle energy that surrounds and interacts with the physical body (Gerber 1988; Hunt 1996). The aura can be seen as a soft glow of light that emanates from a person or object. The glow can be white or it can span the rainbow spectrum of colors. There is no definitive line of separation when healers speak of the finer vibrations of auras, chakras, subtle bodies, and energy fields. The continuum of body-mind-emotions-spirit merges with these fields into other dimensions of being and awareness. It is in this sense that we are said to be multidimensional beings.

EMOTIONS AND
THE ENERGY FIELD

The concept of a reality beyond three dimensions as well as a multidimensional anatomy has long been acknowledged in energy medicine. It can be a mental stretch to comprehend such a realization, however. Let your imagination play with the idea that although we appear to exist in three-dimensional reality, aspects of the atom suggest at least a fourth dimension (Andrews 1966). Most recently, string theory claims that many dimensions exist within the folds of the universe beyond what is perceived with the eye (Greene 2000).

A multidimensional approach to healing embraces the extent to which vocal practices contribute to health. As energetic beings, we extend beyond the physical three-dimensional realm. The voice, too, extends beyond the physical world according to teachings of ancient spiritual traditions such as the Sufis. The vital energy of the living voice carries such creative and transformative emotional power that it can imprint the ethereal spheres with audible and physical impressions (Khan 1988). The voice affects every element of being.

We exist in a living and pulsating environment of light and sound waves, electromagnetic energy, the same stuff of which all life is made. The body contributes to and merges with this electromagnetic field as electrical current is generated through the nervous system, muscles, and cellular activity. According to Hunt (1996), electromagnetic energy contains both high and low frequencies. The magnetic current, associated with healing and tissue health, is very low (less than 100 cycles per second with 0 to 20 cycles per second being typical) and is affected by color. Electrical current, however, is affected by sound and is a very high frequency. It is associated with mind and consciousness (Ibid.). The energy field of the human body is perceived as the aura. The field is continuous, however, and blends with our environment, other people, animals, things. We interact with a universal energy field in a continuous exchange of energy.

The shamanic paradigm holds that the universe is composed of vibrations (Wolf 1992). From this perspective, the finer vibrations are seen as existing in Spirit, in the invisible ethereal realm, while the grosser vibrations exist in matter. The finer invisible realm includes the aura and the energy field. In my mind's eye, I picture a continuum of vibrations where Spirit merges with matter and matter merges with Spirit.

In research lasting more than twenty-five years, Valerie Hunt monitored the "emotions, energy fields, and the neuromuscular effects of Rolfing" (Hunt 1996:22), a form of body-work that involves physical manipulation and stretching. She used a high-frequency telemetry instrument to measure human vibrations. A telemetry instrument is a system designed to intercept and broadcast electrical activity of the body. The instrument used was capable of measuring from 0 to 20,000 cycles per second. Hunt reported that all telemetry recordings included the activity in the aura as well. In addition to the instrument reading of energy, an auric reader, a psychic who can see auras and chakras, reported what she saw occurring in the energy field during Rolfing sessions.

Chakras function in an exchange of energy with the electromagnetic system or aura. Energy also flows between the chakras. Through monitoring the energy centers, Hunt (1996) discovered that each individual has a distinct amplitude and frequency pattern emanating from the chakras and in a synchronous flow of energy between chakras. If a subject reported feeling ill, the instrument readings of the chakras registered anticoherent patterns, an indication that the chakras were not functioning synchronously. The aura was simultaneously described as clouded and muddy by the aura reader. Sound healers report being able to sense when imbalance or anticoherency is present. Their method of restoring a coherent flow of energy is to sound into a person's aura or energy field until they have a sensory image of restored balance.

Hunt (1996) claims that emotions live in the energy field, and it is our emotions that organize the energy field into coherent and anticoherent patterns. As our emotions shift and change, so do the colors in our aura. Each color carries a frequency that emits a sound into the field and changes the energy patterns. Her research indicated "that before the brain wave was activated and before stimuli altered the heart rate, blood pressure or breathing, the field had already responded" (p.25). From this, it was postulated that change first occurs in the "auric field, not in the sensory nerves nor in the brain" (Ibid.). That is, change is initiated in the finer vibrations of the energy field before it occurs in the grosser vibrations of matter that constitute our bodies.

Hunt (1996) made another significant discovery when the brain, heart, and muscle frequencies were removed from the baseline data on the oscilloscope. She found that the field of electromagnetic energy vibrates between eight and ten times faster than the body surface electricity. In addition, she reports that there is a place of quiet, a void, where there is no electrical activity. The quiet space occurs between 250 and 450-500 cycles per second (Ibid.). In other words, there is a silent space between the faster, finer vibrations of the field and the gross vibrations of the physical body.

To suggest that a silent space exists between the frequency of the human body, from 0 to 250 cycles per second, and the frequency of the aura, from about 500 cycles per second up to 20,000 cycles per second (the measurement limit of the instrument used at the time), leads me to wonder about that space of inactivity, the void. The possible existence of such a space requires a leap of faith for the imagination and is inconsistent with the idea of a continuum of vibrations between the gross and the finer mentioned above, between body-mind-emotions-spirit. A continuum as I understand it would indicate no interruption in vibrations; however, there is a silent space according to Hunt, a void where there is no electrical activity in the field. There would appear, then, to be a break in the frequency. My conception of the microtonal space, however, is as a transitional point rather than as a break in the energetic continuum. Given this understanding, the void in the continuum becomes the microtonal space of transition. There is no contradiction in acknowledging the energetic break. Instead, it appears to strengthen my conjecture, which is that healing occurs in the microtonal space.

The void exists as a vacuum. Khan (1988) suggests that the emptiness holds everything, all possibilities. Like the silence, it is a place of unlimited potential. The silent void to which Hunt refers must also be regarded as a place of unlimited potential. This zero point of stillness in between is what I perceive as the microtonal space, possibly comparable to the void of a black hole, which cannot be measured. According to Greene (2000), what occurs at the deepest internal point of a black hole is unknown. It is a mystery. It is a place of transformation at energetic levels. As a transition point, let us acknowledge that, like a vacuum, it holds all possibilities. And it does indeed take a leap of faith to entertain the mystery as a microtonal space of healing. Such faith brings forth the light of hope and love. The healing potential existing in the microtonal space ignites joy in the heart and lights the mysterious realm with boundless possibilities.

My search to understand the concept of microtonal healing led me to microtonal music and microtones, the space between notes. They incite my curiosity. I have no definitive answers, only possible solutions that sometimes offer a tentative moment of comfort in understanding. Such moments are quickly followed by more questions as I notice pieces of information such as those presented in Hunt's (1996) work. My question now is with regard to the void between the body and the energy field. In terms of healing, what is the significance of the space of inactivity that lies within our field of radiance? Based on my theoretical assumption that microtonal healing occurs in the space between, the suggested void is a transformational space between the visible and invisible realms. Change occurs where the two realms are joined by a void between the body and the electromagnetic field.

EMOTIONS AND
THE VOICE

Based on the work of Candace Pert (1999), emotions play a key role in our state of health. She claims that emotions exist within the biochemicals of almost every cell of the body and postulates that emotions are directly linked to the immune system. Within the immune system are monocyte cells that are covered with peptide receptors, biochemicals that hold emotional energy. Further, they are information molecules that direct energy. Perhaps it would be more accurate to state that emotional memories are present within the biochemicals of almost every cell of the body and that those memories are received from the energy field where emotions live. In other words, while the emotions exist in the energy field, emotional memories are held within the cells and are experienced in the body where they can be comprehended.

What does this mean in terms of the healing voice? Singing provides simple access to emotional awareness by way of the breath. The voice is audible breath that stirs emotional memories held in the cells. The undulating microtonal voice in particular elicits deep sentiments that need to surface in order to be acknowledged, soothed, and restored to harmonic resonance. The voice not only directly accesses the emotions, it translates emotional energy into sound. Emotional shifts occurring from moment to moment influence the texture, strength, and clarity of the voice. The voice thus reveals the present emotional state of a person. It conveys the emotional condition at a physically audible level.

The healing voice is multidimensional as is emotional energy. The voice, which carries the emotions, is the vehicle with which to consciously bridge the visible and invisible realms of matter and spirit. Working with the microtonal voice modulates emotions to a place of coherency within the field. It initiates healing and transformation at subtle levels before it becomes manifest in physical reality. In this way, the voice affects the physical well-being of the bodymind by organizing the energy field into coherent patterns. As emotional balance is restored, the voice reflects the internal resonance and harmony of the singer as well as coherency in the energy field.

THE VOICE AND
VOCAL SOUND HEALERS

Vocal sound healers work with the voice as an instrument of healing to restore balance and harmony to body-mind-emotions-spirit. The voice, as an extension of the physical structure in the form of sound, is a personally intimate instrument that reveals a person's state of well-being. The quality of vocal sounds is affected by constant chemical secretions that result from the rise and fall of emotions in response to events and interactions in our daily lives (Newham 1994). The voice reveals emotional blockages in the physical body that need clearing. The body thus becomes audibly perceptible through the voice simultaneously with our normal visual perception. Beaulieu (1987), for example, notices the speaking voice in terms of energetic properties of speed, volume, and pitch. Such vocal nuances are used to evaluate the physical, emotional, and mental states in his clients.

Chanting, singing, and humming internally massage the body and stimulate the release of endorphins. Endorphins increase relaxation, calm the mind, and elevate mood (Goldman 1992; Keyes 1990; Padus 1986). One type of endorphin can mediate pain relief (Gerber 1988). Other physical benefits said to be derived from singing, chanting, and toning include lowering blood pressure and slowing the heart rate (Gardner-Gordon 1993). In addition to accessing emotions, the deep breathing that accompanies vocal practices oxygenates the blood, which increases alertness and the ability to focus and concentrate (Lawlis 1988; Gardner-Gordon 1993).

Sounds that are used to express emotions such as moaning, groaning, yawning, screaming, or crying are referred to as body sounds by Gardner-Gordon (1993) and Garfield (1987). On the other hand, John Beaulieu (1987) calls such body sounds "toning." He suggests that people explore emotions using body sounds; however, he does not indicate, as does Joy Gardner-Gordon (1993), that the use of body sounds for emotional expression can exacerbate pain before relief is experienced. Her suggestion is to go more deeply into the feelings by extending the vocal expressions for an additional five minutes.

People most likely do not want to hear that they might feel worse emotionally or physically before they feel better, but it is important to be aware of possible responses to a sound practice as part of a healing process. Gerber (1988) explains that in the practice of homeopathy, a medical practice that applies principles of energy medicine such as resonance, the frequencies of a person's illness are matched with a microdose of subtle energy. This initially exacerbates a patient's physical illness, thereby creating a healing crisis before balance is restored. It would appear, based on Gardner-Gordon's (1993) statement, that some vocal practices bring a similar response at an emotional or psychological level.

Although those who write about sound healing from a musical theoretical basis refer to resonance (Beaulieu 1987; Gardner 1997; Goldman 1992), the principle of resonance as understood in the practice of energy medicine is not discussed. In other words, an exacerbation of an imbalance might occur in the process of a return to stability. The impression from most literature is that sound healing methods,

27

including vocal sound practices, have only uplifting qualities that are healing in nature. However, Gardner-Gordon (1993) is suggesting something else. A healing crisis that might occur from vocal practices can be psychological in nature, a combination of mental and emotional areas of pain. It would be interesting to notice whether a healing crisis is experienced at a physiological level as a result of using vocal health practices to heal a physical illness or injury.

The usual assumption about the human voice is that, with few exceptions, it has a small range of tonal pitches (Gardner 1997). However, Newham (1994) asserts that the vocal range of the human voice has been limited because people have learned to express intense emotions in words rather than by way of sounds, including animal sounds. To realize optimum potential for self-expression, full use of the voice with all of its emotional nuances is essential. In some cultures, such as the Kaluli in Papua New Guinea (Feld 1994, 1996), the sounds of animals and birds are imitated to evoke emotions. A wide range of sounds with varying degrees of intensity, facial expressions, and physical gestures would be required to generate expressive sounds of fear, joy, and anguish. The potential of the voice has not been widely explored either in range or with regard to healing. With training, people can expand their vocal range in excess of five or six octaves (Newham 1994). If it is true that specific frequencies are needed in the process of healing with sound and if it is true that with training the human voice is capable of sounding multiple octaves, the healing potential of the voice is substantial. The assumption that the human voice has the smallest range of pitches needs to be re-evaluated.

Sound healers refer to a resonant or harmonic state of being when balance exists between body, mind, emotions, and spirit. There is no objective measure to determine balance. It is a subjective perception of well-being. We are sound and sound is a conveyor of energy. The energy has a tangible quality that can be consciously perceived by the senses when we pay attention.

Sound healers sometimes use their own voices to locate an area of imbalance in a person's body. This is done by toning at a person's body beginning at the feet and moving upward to the head to determine the location of illness, disharmony, or an emotional block in energy flow that might be present (Goldman 1992; Gardner 1997). Sounding into a person's body with a siren-like sound or a tone, also called scanning, is similar to echolocation. Gardner (1997) compares the sensation of finding the area where tension or disease is present in the body to the stopping of vocal resonance by placing a hand about two inches from her mouth while sounding. She then sings into the area to release the discomfort.

Feld (1996) tells us that the sounds of the rainforest reveal location to the Kaluli; that is, sound is used to navigate through the forest because vision is obscured by foliage. They listen to the height and depth of sound. Sound is light and dark. It has density. They develop a kinesthetic and sonesthetic awareness because, Feld explains, the Kaluli primarily feel and hear their landscape rather than rely on visual stimuli as they maneuver through the forest. To them, the universe is comprehended and experienced as a living, pulsating environment of vibrational energy. The principle is the same as that used by sound healers to scan the body, noticing differences in texture, heat, and density. A Native American healer described to Wolf (1992), for example, that she perceives a disturbance in the physical body as being thicker and having more density. It is the voice that relays information about a person's well-being, whether it is the person singing or a sound healer using the voice to scan a client's energy.

ETHNOMUSICOLOGY

I turned to the field of ethnomusicology with the hope of better understanding the function of the voice in healing among indigenous cultures. I soon discovered that the focus of research in the ethnomusicology discipline is typically on musical composition, repertories, and social structure within a defined culture. The discipline generally does not address the healing potential of the voice. Nevertheless, some observations of ethnomusicologists are relevant to understanding the function of the healing voice. In my research, I look for common threads that might explain the voice as a creative energy force or material that simply acknowledges the voice as an instrument of healing. Those ethnographies describing the role of song in healing rituals come closest to contributing to the body of knowledge on vocal sound healing.

Because I strive to comprehend why sound heals, I read ethnographies related to healing with music, song, or drum with a new focus. As I delve into ethnographic reports of healing practices in ancient traditions, I search for an approach to music as vibration, an awareness of energy centers of the human body, energy fields, the concept of the universe as vibrational energy composed of sound, the role of sound in creation, and the impact of emotions on the electro-magnetic energy field. These areas of study expand the bound-aries of ethnomusicology in the strict sense of the discipline.

ETHNOMUSICOLOGY
AND EMOTIONS

Indigenous cultures around the world sing and chant to summon emotional energy in a ceremonial context to con-nect with Spirit for healing and transformation. It is emotions that influence the energy field (Hunt 1996). The energy field holds all possibilities for transformation and is where change begins to manifest. This appears to be something traditional-ly acknowledged by indigenous healers in cultures around the world. Shamans and medicine men and women compre-hend a living, pulsating universe at energetic levels. They speak in terms of connecting with the spirits in the invisible realm when they sing and dance to access emotions and arouse what Richard Katz (1982) calls "boiling energy." Steven Feld (1994, 1996) speaks in terms of sentiment, and Marina Roseman (1991) refers to emotional buildup.

In his investigation of the traditional healing practices of the Kalahari !Kung in Africa, Katz (1982) was following his curiosity with regard to understanding the role of con-sciousness in healing. His ethnography provides a solid foun-dation from which to glimpse the role of consciousness, emo-tions, and song in healing. His description of the healing process details the function of energy rising and falling in the form of num. Num is the life force, referred to as Chi in Chinese medicine. The Kalahari !Kung healers activate the healing energy of num through song and dance to effect individual and community healing. Num lives in the songs; however, num requires dance for healing. The num songs are sung from the heart and carry emotional energy.

Both Feld and Roseman are ethnomusicologists. Their focus is on the music, song, and dance of healing rituals in a cultural context. In discussing the ceremonies of the Temiar in the Malaysian Rainforest, Marina Roseman (1991) describes the two-toned pulsing rhythms produced by stamping bamboo tubes and drumming. The pulsation alternates between high and low frequencies. Such sounds resemble the sounds of nature and activate emotional longing and subsequent release during the ceremonial performance. Additionally, swaying motions intensify the emotional content of song for the Temiar (Roseman 1991). Emotional buildup is presented as descriptive of the ritual rather than as functional in the healing itself. The similitude I notice with accounts of the Temiar and !Kung healing ceremonies is the emotional buildup through movement and song followed by release. Similarly, Feld (1994, 1996) reports a primary element in the song of the Kaluli as being emotional sentiment. Emotional longing and sentiment are said to be related to the calling of spirits or connecting with spirits in the invisible realm.

As an anthropologist who has not directly experienced the healing practices of indigenous cultures such as the !Kung, Temiar or Kaluli, I rely on ethnographers such as Feld, Katz, and Roseman in my effort to comprehend the energetic impact of emotions and vocal sounds in healing and transformation. I am indebted to them for their ethnographic reports of healing ceremonies.

Observations of healing ceremonies described in ethno-graphies open doors of speculation and expand comprehension of the healing efficacy of the voice. Common threads do present themselves in the reports of curing performances. For now, I can only speculate as to the function of emotional buildup in the healing rituals. Based on Katz's description, I am inclined to believe that emotional longing among the Temiar and sentiment of the Kaluli serve to activate healing energy or life force as it does for the !Kung.

Some commentaries on healing songs of indigenous cultures do shed a glimmer of hope onto my work by alluding to microtones. However, they do not tell us how or why microtones are used, they only describe their musical quality. Powers (1992), for example, describes the Oglala vocalization of prayer as microtonal in that it occasionally rises an octave or more in microtonic steps from a low vocal tone. This corresponds with the cascading patterns of their traditional singing. In a similar fashion, Charles Briggs (1996) analyzes the musical structure of a Warao healing song in Venezuela. He notices a rise and fall within a melodic contour that climbs to a high pitch before sliding downward on a glissando. This can be compared to sliding down the strings of a harp or along a piano keyboard in one stroke. There is no speculation as to what extent these singing patterns contribute to the healing power of the song.

Much of what is occurring is what I call microtonal. It occurs between the visible and invisible realms and escapes notice. It slips past what is perceptible to the five senses. There is more going on in healing performances than ethnomusicologists are trained to discern. Because the emotions impact the energy field, and it is in the field that physical change first begins to manifest (Hunt 1996), the buildup of emotional energy takes on added significance with regard to the process of healing in these cultures.

MICROTONAL HEALING

To my knowledge, there is no discussion of microtonal healing in any vocal sound healing literature; however, some references do suggest that microtones were used to effect healing transformation at one time. The Harvard Dictionary of Music (Apel 1973) indicates that ragas were believed to have magical powers to heal disease. Gardner (1997) states that we need to reclaim the healing power of music such as that found in ragas and the healing melodic modes used by Pythagoras. The microtonal quality once a part of Greek music became lost in the development of Western music as we know it today (Gardner 1997; Danielou 1995). Even though these sources suggest that microtonal music could have been used for purposes of healing, a link between healing and the emotional nature of singing micro-tones is not specifically indicated. An understanding of this link is essential if we are to comprehend the function of the voice in the healing process.

The application of microtonal musical concepts goes beyond a musical theory based on harmonics to explain the healing voice. Microtonal concepts are thus offered here as another lens through which to perceive healing processes in general and vocal healing in particular. Where harmonics tend to lead an explorer into the invisible realm and the laws

34

of the universe, microtonal concepts return us to the flow of life on Earth. We need to recognize the living force in sounds of the human voice and the sounds of nature. Where harmonics and microtones meet is the space between. It is there that we will find a theoretical foundation that supports the healing voice.

2
MICROTONAL SINGING

HONORING YOUR
SINGING VOICE

If you find it a great challenge allowing yourself to sing freely, you are not alone. The singing voice is often the mode of expression that people are discouraged from using at an early age. Many people grow up believing that they cannot sing. Such silencing of expression is gradually internalized until a person becomes embarrassed or even ashamed of the sound of his or her own singing. In some instances, even the speaking voice is disparaged. In addition to being discouraged from singing, we have not been trained to work with the voice as an instrument of healing. Such education is not part of our cultural heritage. The voice is the most natural tonal instrument for healing available to us. It lives within us from the moment of birth.

The basic Do Re Mi scale as it is taught to children in the United States is absent of microtones as well as flat and sharp notes. The scale is taught in whole notes, and this nonfluctuation of the perfect singing voice follows most people into adulthood. Some are classified as "alto" with voices to harmonize, but they will seldom be permitted to honor their singing voice alone. The accompanying message is that unless you can sing those pure whole tones precisely, you can't sing. Judgment of the voice stifles the joy of singing. Thus develops a pattern of silencing a natural and healing form of expression.

I remember laughing out loud for the first time when I was thirty years old. The sound of my own laughter caught me off guard. It sounded strange to hear myself laugh. Until that day, my laughter had been a muffled sound, barely a whispered breath behind a closed smile. Today, my laughter is spontaneous and audible. I recognize it as the sound of my humor, a unique sound as it is for every individual. Singing was another challenge.

It was June 1993 in an expressive arts therapy class that I was first exposed to the concept of healing with voice. Giving vocal expression to an emotional state was an experiential assignment for the class. I was at a point in my life when long-suppressed anger was bubbling to the surface. I didn't feel safe enough to sound the full force of my emotions. My emotional sounds were not the love and peace of the new age era they once had been. Participation in the vocal exercise at the next class was mandatory or I would not pass the course. I felt as if I was teetering on the edge of an abyss. The class was scheduled to resume in two days, and I knew I had to deal with sounding. After some deliberation, I decided to bring my dragon hand puppet to class to serve as a vehicle for my sound. I had no idea what the sound might be.

Perhaps giving myself the choice of sounding through the dragon puppet provided me with a safety net. I arrived at class dreading the moment of having to sound my emotions but confident my dragon could safely do so even if it roared and breathed fire. Much to my relief, the instructor gave us options. We could work alone or with a partner, and we could sound our emotional state or bring forth a healing sound. I opted to work with a partner and together we chose to elicit healing sounds from Spirit. It felt safe because to my conscious mind, a healing sound had nothing to do with emotions. There was no need to let the dragon roar. Nevertheless, there was still an element of apprehension.

I had never been called on to sound a tone or to release my singing voice in front of a group of people. Then I remembered a time when I was ten years old and camping with a neighborhood playmate, Suzie, and her family. Not far from camp, a huge rock that was prominently positioned amid the fragrance of forest pines had become our favorite singing place. Each day, we climbed up to the flat surface of the rock where we sat cross-legged and sang "On Top of Old Smokey" at the top of our lungs, Suzie in a high soprano voice that I tried to match.

In class, I closed my eyes and mentally went back to that time. From that space, unaware of the classmates who surrounded us, I was able to vocalize a sound with the woman who sat on the carpeted floor across from me. Beautiful sounds seemed to rise up from deep within like nothing I expected or ever could have imagined. Our tones, long and sustained, merged. Tones, as if from singing bowls, enveloped me sending sonorous vibrations through me. The door to singing opened for me that day. My fear of vocal sounding lay at my feet in a puddle of shimmering light. The beauty of healing sounds was nothing to be feared after all. They rose up from the earth along with a wonderful childhood memory. Today, I sing every day.

I have come to realize that it requires a tremendous amount of energy to resist flowing with the natural rhythm of life. Resistance creates tension and tension is reflected in the voice when expression of your life force is disregarded in the moment. To physically and energetically experience the effect of resistance, make the tiniest vocal tone you can. Make it a short burst of tone, a tiny creak, minuscule in duration, a dot of sound. Notice the vocal restraint required in emitting the tiniest of sounds. Notice, too, that the tone cannot remain restricted once the sound is initiated. At some point, the tiny burst of vocalization requires extension and can become somewhat like the sound of a mosquito. In extended form, the tone tends to waver and flicker and then fades away. Releasing physical and emotional tension can begin in this way. Always remember that the healing is in the microtonal space, even in a dot of sound.

Every person has the gift of a natural pitch, a voice that reflects the beauty within. The voice is the natural sound of the body. It is the source of a person's healing (Khan 1988, 1996). This is why it is so important for vocal sound healers to teach others to use their own voices for healing. Your voice signals your state of well-being by accessing information about your mental, physical, emotional, and spiritual health. It gives external expression to internalized life experiences and processes. Essentially, we are seeking a return to that which is natural, to a homeostasis on every level using the voice as a guide.

The purpose of vocal healing practices is to enhance and maintain your state of well-being. The process is one of conscious listening and working with the voice intuitively while allowing healing sounds, tones, overtones, and microtones to evolve. Vocal healing practices offer a continuous awakening that progresses from day to day. The benefits are more immediately experienced with your own singing because you are the sound source. Each day, you go a little further, your depth of understanding increases, and your awareness expands.

Vocal sounds are audible symbols of internal emotional states that waver and flutter in and out of awareness. The healing power of the voice lies in connecting deeply with the emotional energies of the moment. It is a direct, firsthand experience in which you are developing an intimate relationship with your own voice by coming to know and appreciate the tonal qualities that emanate from within. You are conducting an inquiry with your voice, an exploration of your resonant well-being.

To begin, create a special healing space in your home where you will not be disturbed and where you feel free to explore your voice. You can think of it as your vocal meditative space, a sacred space to honor your voice as a connection to Spirit, God, or Higher Guidance. Your space can include a small altar to hold a votive candle, crystals, and other healing symbols that provide support in your process.

Learning to use the sound of your own voice consciously can begin with the smallest sound and blossom from there. The goal is not to exhibit vocal talent or perfection. The goal is to unfetter the voice, which has been limited to fit vocal standards. When I teach people to sing and chant, we begin with one word, one sound, a soft hum, or a single syllabic tone. These are natural, simple sounds. Nevertheless, it can take courage to emit a vocal sound. As one student of microtonal singing discovered, vocalization takes up space in a room. It announces your presence. Honoring the sound of your voice is an indication of more comfort with taking up space in the world of everyday living.

For those who are new to singing for the purpose of healing, you most likely have not explored your voice with what I call "conscious abandon." When you are free sounding with conscious abandon, there is no room for judgment. Be patient with yourself as you begin your vocal exploration. As your first sound is made, listen without judgment. There is no right or wrong. There is only audible breath with a frequency range of tonal expression that is unique to you and your physical structure. It is your voice. Whether pure tones ring forth or not is unimportant. What is important is that you are sounding. Trust that whatever vocal sound emerges is perfect. You are learning to use the sound of your voice to give expression to your state of well-being and to restore and maintain balance.

The journey of the healing voice has a unique landscape with a distinct vibrational texture for each person. Your responses to microtonal singing, overtone chanting, toning, humming, and vocable expression are specific to your process and life experiences. It is only through exploring your own vocal sounds that you can fully grasp the power of these practices to shape and transform your life.

Everyone experiences sound differently, and your own experiences are what will hold significance and meaning for you. A process of relational being with yourself, your environment, and with others unfolds as your singing voice is experienced internally and externally. You have only to pay attention to your body while sounding to experience the vibrations through your skeletal structure and in the air around you generated by these practices. Eventually, the power of the living voice to nurture healthful well-being becomes a conscious reality and way of life. Singing enlivens the breath of Spirit within your body. Let your voice fly and Spirit will soar with you.

MICROTONES AND THE MUSIC OF NORTH INDIA

My introduction to microtonal singing came about through the study of the classical music of North India with Silvia Nakkach. She provided me with a basic understanding of music theory based on raga form and guided me in finding my microtonal voice. The technical information on Indian music described below is primarily from my study with her.

The piano has proved to be a helpful visual reference in my quest to comprehend music theory in general and classical Indian music theory in particular. The black keys on the piano keyboard express halftones called sharps and flats. The same black key can be both C sharp and D flat. The fact that one key can have two values gives rise to the term "diatonic" in western music. It is also the black keys that represent the microtones in Indian ragas; that is, they indicate where microtones occur. They are not the microtonal notes.

Music is related to the tuning of an instrument. Western music is based on the tuning of the piano, with a scale of twelve tones, five of which are called halftones. The notes played on a piano are consistent. They do not vary. Given its construction, nothing smaller than a halftone can be played on a piano unless it is specifically tuned to produce microtones. Microtones are notes that live between the keys on a

45

piano. The voice, stringed instruments, and wind instruments can access them.

India's musical history dates back at least five thousand years. The musical language of Hindus grew out of their religious beliefs. Their music flows from the sacred Sanskrit text of the Vedic scriptures. The solfege (Sa Re Ga ma Pa Dha Ni Sa) represent deities, a discussion of which is beyond the scope of this book.

Neither the music of the West nor the English vocabulary has the capacity to describe the characteristics of Indian music. For this reason, there are immediate problems in translating Indian musical terms. Indian music, with a scale of twenty-two tones, originally arose from the experience of singing. Second, their music was created after the tuning of their stringed instruments. With stringed instruments, the tones are not separate from each other. The point where one note ends and another begins is not easily defined. The notes move and change. The twenty-two tones in the Indian scale are of two different types. Svaras (pronounced shwaras) are a series of five, six, or seven notes that do not change. The rest of the notes are called srutis (pronounced shruties).

According to the Sanskrit text, srutis are the smallest intervals perceived by the ear (Tagore 1874). Srutis, or microtones, are the heart of Hindu music. Unlike svaras, srutis change. They are heard as a fluttering of notes rather than as a stable tone. Microtones are the intervalic connective tissue that fills the spaces between the stable svaras. The stable tones are held together or connected by srutis. Microtonal singing gives rise to cultivating the art of connecting the notes, referred to as meend in North Indian music (Mathieu 1997).

The richness of Indian classical music resides in the spaces between notes, in the srutis or microtones. They form the basis for the Hindu musical system (Tagore 1874). Srutis cannot be uniformly quantified as quarter notes because the value of srutis shifts depending on where they arise within a raga. Some srutis are third tones. They cannot be pinned down to one or the other. They are both. They evolve and unfold each time the notes are played or sung. Svaras, or basic tones, are defined whole notes, whereas srutis emerge from the spaces between svaras and cannot be contained, defined, or predetermined. This is because they arise from that place of mystery, a fluctuating emotional space in the moment.

To permit intellectual quantification of an emotional and psychic phenomenon denies and invalidates its living power. Because srutis are felt at an emotional level, to attempt to rationalize them is to lose touch with the inherent emotionality that calls them forth musically. One does not think about performing microtones. They simply float to the surface, riding on the breath or on the vibrational energy of the string. They are inherent in the instrument of the voice, and they are reproduced especially with stringed instruments like the vina or sitar. Only after they are performed can srutis be noted.

The voice was the first musical instrument, and it is from the voice that the srutis emerged (Tagore 1874). At the time, music was not written down. This tradition continues as a student of Hindu music learns to hear and feel the srutis by listening to and imitating his teacher. The student becomes acquainted with the sounds internally, at a feeling level, by using the voice before learning to reproduce the sounds on a musical instrument.

47

Again, there is no comparable terminology in the music of the West for some aspects of Indian music. Growing up in the United States, I learned a whole-note musical scale (C-D-E-F-G-A-B-C) with the accompanying solfege Do Re Mi Fa Sol La Ti Do. I assumed it was the only scale there was and did not question that there might be others. In Indian classical music, there are ten basic scales called the "10 Thats" (pronounced Tats). The 10 Thats are also referred to as ragas. There are seventy-two ragas from which close to thirty-five thousand scales are derived, and there is a possibility for about ninety-two thousand (Lentz 1961).

Raga has no English equivalent. A raga can best be described as a melodic pattern, but it is something more. Although a raga does consist of a series of notes, the notes also flutter and slide with a luminous glow of life. They generate colorful strands of emotions that weave meaning into the heart of the moment (Menon 1974). Western mind is challenged to acknowledge an aspect of music that escapes capture or definition in its musical terminology. It is only in the practicing of the ragas that their nature and power can be absorbed. They must be integrated into the psychic structure of the singer for comprehension to occur.

The first three raga scales, Bhairava (pronounced By-rav), Bilawal (pronounced Billa-wall), and Bhairavi (pronounced By-ravee) are shown in Figure 1 below. For simplicity in identifying the notes of these ragas, middle C has been assigned to Sa. In the classical music of North India, however, Sa can be any note. To distinguish svaras from srutis in written music, svaras are written with capital letters. Srutis are written with lowercase letters to indicate that the note is sung microtonally with a vocal flutter. On a piano, assume that Sa is the note C, Re is D, and re (written in low-ercase to indicate the occurrence of a sruti) is represented by D flat. The sruti re is more than D flat, however. It is the two or three microtones between C and E. Srutis are flexible. They connect the stable svaras with emotional threads when they are sung.

Bhairava
[5:00 a.m. – 11:00 a.m.]

Musical Notes:	C	Db	E	F	G	Ab	B	C
	Sa	re	Ga	ma	Pa	dha	Ni	Sa

Bilawal
[11:00 a.m. – 12:00 noon and all day]

Musical Notes:	C	D	E	F	G	A	B	C
	Sa	Re	Ga	ma	Pa	Dha	Ni	Sa

Bhairavi
[12:00 noon, afternoon and at midnight]

Musical Notes:	C	Db	Eb	F	G	Ab	Bb	C
	Sa	re	ga	ma	Pa	dha	ni	Sa

Figure 1

There are between two and four srutis for each note written in lowercase, depending on where they occur within the raga. For example, re is two or three srutis, whereas ma and dha can contain three or four srutis. In actuality, micro-tonal notes are either flat or sharp, depending on whether the flow of the scale is up or down. The exception is ma. Although ma is always microtonal, the F note is natural.

Indian music can only be comprehended through the practice and exploration of singing. It is a lifelong practice that embodies a philosophy of being, a way of life that acknowledges the world as a place of process and flux. There is a point in practicing Indian music when silence enters the space naturally and envelops the singer. It calls attention to listening to internal rhythms and to noticing the movement between sound and silence. It becomes an art of maintaining balance between silence and singing and, in the process, coming to know when to listen and when to speak. It is an example of music reflecting balance in communication.

In the same way that it is necessary to know when to speak and when to remain silent, classical Indian music has specific ragas or melodic patterns for different times of the day. They are related to cosmology and the movement of light. It is important to sing or play the appropriate raga for the specific time of day so that the spirit of the srutis, or micro-tones, really shines.

The first morning raga, Bhairava (Sa re Ga ma Pa dha Ni Sa), is sung between 5:00 a.m. and 11:00 a.m. It connects the strands of consciousness when the mind is just waking up and is very flexible. The srutis (re ma dha) are woven between the stable svaras (Sa Ga Pa Ni). Bhairava is a gentle awaken-ing that sets the tone for flowing through the day, so to speak.

Bilawal (Sa Re Ga ma Pa Dha Ni Sa), which is more steady, reflects a more stable and awake consciousness that occurs from 11:00 a.m. to 12:00 noon and all day. Only ma is expressed in srutis. I perceive this as maintaining a sense of playfulness and flexibility between the balance of the stable svaras. Bilawal is about being awake, aware, and whole.

It reflects joyfulness and opening. That is its healing quality and it can be sung during the entire day.

To arrive at Bhairavi, we need to travel through the first two morning ragas. Bhairava is associated with the right brain and Bilawal with the left brain. Bhairava tends to awaken creative thought processes which, according to Zdenek (1983), are thought to arise from activity of the right hemisphere of the brain. Bilawal stimulates comprehension and stabilizes mental focus, which are attributed to the logical left hemisphere of the brain (Ibid.). These ragas are synchronous, one helping the other. They prepare the way to enter the emotional space of Bhairavi.

It is no coincidence that Bhairavi (Sa re ga ma Pa dha ni Sa), the most microtonal of all ragas, has its place in the heat of the day from 12:00 noon and into the afternoon, as if to reflect and embrace emotional warmth. The emotions of Bhairavi are reflected again after midnight in the light of the stars. Bhairavi is a high-energy raga that provides a direct connection with Spirit. It invites relaxation into a devotional protection.

The emotional content of raga form music is not surprising given that rag means color in Sanskrit and is said to generate emotions in the human heart (Titon 1984). It is inherent in this music to evoke emotions. The tender heart transforms a tone into a semitone, and as the heart becomes softer and more tender, the tone blossoms into microtones (Khan 1988). In my experience, emotional awareness surfaces in the delicate singing. Emotions are stirred from a nonverbal place. Emotions ride on the fluttering voice and can easily slide into resonance or enter into a still point between.

MICROTONAL SINGING
AS A HEALING PRACTICE

M icrotonal singing is a gentle vocal practice that offers an intuitive approach to healing with the voice. It is a specific form of singing that manipulates the voice to produce microtonal sounds as an experiential process of discovery and potential healing. The classical raga form music of Northern India serves as a beginning point for singing microtonally; however, I stray from raga form for purposes of healing.

The raga scales offer an outline of form and structure for the microtonal voice. To assist students in their independent practice, I give them a five-by-eight card with the first three ragas: Bhairava, Bilawal, and Bhairavi (see Figure 1). Using the raga chart helps to identify the whole notes, distinguishing them from the flat and sharp notes that are sounded microtonally. You might want to create such a reference for yourself to keep in your singing practice space or on your altar. A piano or electronic keyboard can serve as a guide in hearing and sounding the correct notes for each raga.

An electronic keyboard is also useful in providing a stable backdrop of harmony to support the microtonal voice. Harmony, in the western sense of the term, is not possible in Indian music because the microtones change too suddenly and the notes are never consistently the same. Harmony is provided as a drone, a continuous interval of sound against which srutis are identifiable. It supports the melody of the raga and allows the shimmering microtones to glisten. A suitable drone can be attained on an electronic keyboard by setting it to pipe organ and playing a sustained fifth (C and G) or a sustained fourth (C and F). You can also use a sruti box, a bellows-type instrument available from music stores specializing in musical instruments from India.

Be kind to your voice by initiating your practice session using your natural breath voice. This is done by sounding "ahh" or other soft vowel sound such as "ooh" in a single tone. Trust the tone that comes forth as you begin. Move into sounding Sa in a single tone. Continue your vocalization of Sa until your tone feels solid and firm. From there, bend the sound into an easy slide upward and then bend it back in a downward slide. The sliding voice also holds microtones. Singing even one note in a microtonal slide to another note is beneficial. Notice your response to bending a note upward and then to bending a note downward. There is no right or wrong response. There is only the personal response of each individual.

When you are ready, choose a raga scale that feels appropriate and comfortable for the time of day. Warm up your voice until it is gliding up and down the scale with ease. Sing in small solfege progressions up the raga scale: Sa Re Ga followed by Sa Re Ga ma to the next progression Sa Re Ga ma Pa and continuing until you reach Sa in the next octave. Then sing in a similar fashion back down the scale in small progressions to the beginning Sa. You may not realize how far you have gone until you return home to Sa (middle C).

In learning to produce microtones, remember that they are inherent in the instrument of the voice. Practice wavering your voice on a note. Then flutter your voice into a microtonal vibration. This exercise helps the voice acquire a delicate and refined strength. It is also useful as a form of vocal exploration. Take as much time as you need to become comfortable with your microtonal voice. Then begin singing up and down the raga scale, inserting microtones in the appropriate spaces. Continue singing in this fashion until you feel a sense of ease in connecting the stable notes with microtones. Some find it easier to produce microtones singing up the scale. Others experience more ease sounding microtones while singing down the scale. Notice your response to the practice at the end of each session. You might want to keep a journal specifically for that purpose.

With practice, wavering and fluttering your voice will deepen your experience and understanding of the microtonal healing process. The more you work with your microtonal voice the more its sonorous texture is revealed. Sensitivity to the healing quality of microtones becomes heightened. You might begin to experience the microtonal notes as food for the soul. Sometimes between Pa and dha or between ni and Sa there can be a sense of reaching for something more, the great longing for connection with your Eternal Self or Spirit. At these points, sliding upward to the next note can bring a sense of relief. Then, descending the scale with microtones and slides, returning to Sa (middle C), brings you back into your body. You might feel as if you have returned home to a grounded place with your feet firmly planted on the earth.

It is not necessary to follow a scale in your daily practice sessions. You are free to use raga scales or not. You can work with Sa re Ga or other solfege progressions exclusively for a time. You can skip notes, singing Sa Pa Sa or any other combination repeatedly. Develop a relationship with each note, with each small solfege progression or combination. You might notice different emotions being stirred or freed by singing in this manner. It is not uncommon to work on one grouping of solfege for a week, a month, or even a lifetime.

Punctuate your vocal practice session with brief moments of silence following a microtonal quaver, a stable tone, or a microtonal slide. Notice your responses to the srutis, svaras, and the silence. Remaining in the silence can take you deeply into your process where intuitive insights are within reach. Practice ending a musical phrase on a note that sounds unfamiliar or unfinished and notice how it feels. It might sound dissonant or unnatural because in the western musical tradition, there is a sound of completion to a musical phrase or a song. The ear is trained to understand some notes as the conclusion. You are encouraged to explore all of these options. Go where your voice takes you and pay attention to your experiences and responses. In any case, return home to Sa at the end of your session to ground yourself.

Rather than singing the Sa Re Ga solfege, you can choose to sing free-form melodic patterns sounding soft vowels and inserting microtones where your voice guides you to do so. As a student of microtonal singing, you are encouraged to let your tones emerge and meander spontaneously. The tones and microtones simply present themselves, opening the precise and appropriate space to take you where you need to be emotionally, mentally, physically, and spiritually. With free-form microtonal singing, there is no predetermined formula to follow. The searching voice wanders, allowing intuitive processes to serve as a guide. There is freedom to sing one note, to sing a fluttering of microtones, to slide from one note to another, and to pause periodically to enter the silence. You will discover that the formless structure of microtonal singing is flexible, flowing, rippling, wavering, and sometimes still.

More than any other vocal healing practice, microtonal vocalizations are propelled by the emotionality that lingers in the cellular structure of the body. The body holds emotional memories, and microtones access emotions and bring them to conscious awareness. The voice can reveal where you are holding emotions and have lost flexibility. You might experience specific tones where they are needed in different parts of your body. Pay attention to the visceral feeling messages that your emotions carry.

Emotions are a condition of being human. They rise and fall, ebb and flow, shift and transform. Emotions can float past awareness with an elusive quality that defies recognition or capture. Yet it is emotions that give meaning and content to our lives. They shape our psyche and impress our presence not only on the world but also in the electromagnetic field. Emotional energy is always present and being dealt with at some level, sometimes more intensely than other instances.

It has been my experience that emotions bring thoughts to the surface. The natural relay of emotion to thought is so fleeting that we are fooled into believing that the process is one of the mind bringing forth emotions. While it is possible to think about something and summon an emotion, it is a two-way street, and we typically ignore that our emotions elicit thought patterns.

Emotional content is not necessarily part of the healing process, however. Emotions are initially nonverbal experiences that are translated into words as we attempt to understand them. We try to give emotions a rational context by verbalizing something beyond words. In working with the microtonal voice, the essence of the emotion is accessed. We elicit the heart of feelings, pure emotions, deep and verbally inexpressible. Staying with pure emotions for as long as possible is encouraged in the microtonal process. Transformation occurs as your voice is intuitively guided to restore a sense of harmonic well-being. Insights may float to the surface through this nonverbal process, but it is not a necessary aspect of healing. Healing with the microtonal voice is something more.

It is in the nature of microtones to initiate transformation. Healing consciously begins with the slightest movement induced with microtonal vibrations of the voice. The microtonal voice is the vehicle for accessing the space where rich emotional landscapes nestle between awaiting vocal expression. The process is one of actively engaging with and entering the microtonal space. As the microtonal singing voice dips in and out of the space between notes, emotions are roused to movement and given expression.

Microtones evolve and unfold anew with each singing because they arise from an emotional space that is continuously shifting throughout the day. Microtones both reflect and accommodate emotional shifting. They ripple on the breath in a subtle grammar that fluctuates from moment to moment. Through their rich yet delicate textures and shapes, microtones reveal our emotional nature. The voice wavers and wanders, searching for something as yet undefined, something that lives in the mystery, in the space between. It tugs at pure emotions that are seeking acknowledgment.

The flexibility of microtonal singing allows for the flow of the voice in the moment, making the movement toward healthful balance inherent in the practice. Working together in a complementary manner, the stable svaras and the microtonal srutis hold the essence of healing between them. They accommodate and encourage both change and stability. The quavering microtonal voice lingers in the space, modulating and soothing emotional energy into alignment and balance. At that point, the voice moves naturally to a place of stability and sounds a clear and solid tone. When you sound a clear, pure tone, cultivate it. Breathe it in. Resonate with it. Enjoy it and know that it is affirming alignment of your energy on every level of being.

If you begin on a whole, full tone, insert microtones and notice where it takes you. Cultivate the srutis. They can be joyous and emotionally uplifting. Fluff your emotions with srutis and then return to a fully resonant and clear tone. Practice perfecting the art of meending by allowing the srutis to serve as an energetic bridge to connect the notes. Sing some microtones then slide into a place where you can join with a solid tone, a svara. Sounding a stable tone periodically in the microtonal singing process will take you to a secure place of grounding. This is a method of anchoring yourself, before proceeding further.

Sliding the voice upward from one clear and stable tone to another and then sliding back down is a healing and bene-ficial microtonal practice in and of itself. The healing aspect of the microtonal slide is that it provides a clear and simple path for resonance to find its way. It is also an emotionally easy practice. As the voice glides up and down between notes, it clears a path with precise emotionality, creating a union along the continuum of body-mind-emotions-spirit. The microtonal slide restructures and strengthens harmonic well-being, mending any tears in your auric field by gently nudging your vibrational patterns into shimmering, coherent resonance.

The rippling microtonal voice conveys an emotional language of the soul, a feeling language of the heart that stimulates a realization of one consciousness of being. Microtonal singing can stimulate transcendental processes that transport consciousness to a blissful state as the voice becomes fluid. Intertwining matter with the cosmos, translucent strands of liquid tone create sound weavings that elicit deep emotional meaning for the singer. Emotional dimensions spill forth in an array of improvised tones as the voice displays a tonal dance of kaleidoscopic colors. Each tonal dance renders a sense of being uplifted and carried by Spirit on multicolored luminescent threads. The fabric of the microtonal voice gives sonorous form to inner dimensions of pure emotions while connecting the physical bodymind with the luminous body-mind. Microtonal singing soon becomes a conscious and meaningful practice of working with the multidimensional emotional energy of the visible and invisible worlds.

Embark on your sonorous journeys trusting that your voice is linked to Spirit. Allow your voice to guide you in the process of transformation and healing. The microtonal space is malleable, and its characteristic flow naturally entices a return to resonant well-being. Listen as you elicit audible emotional form with your singing voice. With practice, you will come to recognize your voice as an extension of your physical and emotional presence. Notice how your emotional self can be soothed, shaped, and ultimately allowed to blossom with the flexibility of microtones fluctuating upward, downward, inward, outward, or in a spiraling or circular configuration.

Working consciously with the microtonal voice accelerates the return to balance. Imagine yourself being sculpted by the sounds and rhythms you bring forth. It is in the nature of microtones to accommodate the voice in bending, fluttering, and sliding naturally into higher frequencies of resonant well-being. You can bend and shape and smooth the rough edges of your emotional contours by using conscious vocal maneuvers. Sing the moment. Sing the space as you are moved to do so.

Silence as well as microtones reside in the spaces between notes. In the course of singing, it is both the microtones and the silence that access emotions. The emotional power of microtones arises from the silent spaces in which they dwell. The duration of the space, whether it is a place of silence or microtones, determines the depth of the emotional experience. Singing the space prepares the way to enter the silence. In the process of singing, consciousness flies between the notes too and enters a still point of awareness in the silence. When the voice enters the silence, awareness follows.

Allow yourself a silent space, a pause, in your microtonal singing. When you merge with the silence, it holds steady and quiets the mind. Singing and stopping between notes is a reminder that between the chaos of daily activities, there is a space of quiet and calm. It becomes a safe and comforting place where the silence is a calming container for all of the activities of the day. Stop at different points during your singing practice to insert silence in unexpected or unusual places such as midway going up the scale, after a microtonal expression, or after a full, round tone. Notice how vibrations from your singing linger in the air as if they are finding a place to nestle in the silence. Once settled into the silence, the lingering vibrations comfort and calm the energy of the place.

In the form of silence, the space between the notes produces a state of suspension, one in which there is no anticipation of the next note. Freedom from anticipation and expectation allows more freedom for the voice to travel and fly. Entering the silence from a point of not knowing and with a sense of sweet abandon and trust prepares you to explore a realm of possibilities with your voice. Leaving expectations behind, you are prepared to sing colors of fluid motion and to paint outside of the lines with your microtonal voice.

You will begin to notice that you sing solid tones periodically as it feels appropriate. You also stop singing when and where you need to stop because there is a sense of completion that comes with microtonal singing. A session can be as brief as five minutes or it can continue for thirty minutes or more. You know when you arrive at the right place, one that is perfect for the moment. You enter the stillness. Stability presents itself.

In a world of microtonal movement, stability, like everything else in the universe, is momentary. Stability is also relative to the individual person or life form. The hummingbird, for example, flutters its wings in a whir to remain stable midair while drinking nectar from a flower. The microtonal flutter allows you to drink the nectar of your emotions in the moment. There can be a sense of stability in the microtonal flutter because in sounding srutis, you are sounding the moment and acknowledging where you are. The microtonal note blossoms into a bouquet of tones that flutters with emotional pollen to seed insights about life processes.

Microtonal singing teaches us about ourselves in practical and meaningful ways. One student of microtonal singing noticed that there were times when her voice cracked. The cracking in her voice occurred when she tried to hold her natural vocal fluttering still. She came to understand the cracking in her singing voice not as a flaw but as a sruti trying to be free. Translating her cracking voice into a sruti came to evoke a place of humor and elicit a sense of freedom for her. Rather than setting out with an intention of where her singing would go, it allowed her to abandon preconceived ideas and to simply observe what developed. That is the microtonal process.

Any vocal sounds that are perceived as imperfections in the process of microtonal singing or while engaging in any vocal healing practice serve as a guide. The so-called vocal imperfections are perfect expressions of your internal state. What is perceived as an imperfection is a point of entry to a healing place. Allow your voice to hang out in the space of imperfection with lighthearted humor. Acknowledge your natural vocal qualities as strengths. By striving for perfection, you stand in your own way of flowing freely. In honoring your voice, you honor your place in the world and come to realize that you have been singing a song of perfection all along.

There are times when I enjoy the dissonance of a flat note. It adds color to an otherwise uneventful moment. It also helps develop the ability to hear what would normally be tuned out. Microtonal singing is a practice that can develop tolerance, understanding, and appreciation of something out of the ordinary, something different from that which has been acclaimed as correct and is moving beyond what has been termed "harmony" in our culture.

As you continue to honor and explore your voice with microtonal singing, you begin to relax rigid images of yourself in the world. Allowing your essence to shine through your singing voice brings acceptance of who you are deep within. It brings intimate knowledge of the voice as a direct link to Spirit.

Experiential exploration of microtones can teach us how to live in balance and harmony by flowing with the natural rhythm of life. Placing the flow of life in a microtonal context offers a musical structure with which to consider the healing process. Microtonal singing reflects that process. Take every opportunity to develop your microtonal singing voice and you will invite transformation from the heart of your innermost being.

3
MICROTONAL CONCEPTS

CONTEXTUALIZING MICROTONES

Living in a predominantly visual society, microtonal concepts come to life for us when demonstrated in shape, form, color, texture, and the space between. This section explores the relational aspects of microtonal concepts for the purpose of reframing perceptions of life experiences. Understanding the relational aspects of microtones sheds light on living in the between space. Microtones exist in relationship, as do we. Each person is a microtonal being. As such, we are the interval and more. We are the glue in relational being with self, other, and environment.

The between space includes the intervalic connection in relationships. For example, I had the opportunity to conduct a six-week study of library story time as a community. What caught my attention were the relational aspects of story-time participants. I perceived the children as active listeners existing between the story and the storyteller. At other times, it seemed the storyteller was the glue connecting the children and the story. She became animated with the life of the story in the telling of it. Or was the story the microtonal aspect of the triad? It soon became clear that the children, the storyteller, and the story composed a musical chord. Together, they became the microtonal aspects of story time that made it a cohesive event.

Examining your life from your position in the microtonal space adds a living dimension to place in family, community, and the world. Imagine yourself existing in the microtonal space in a relational situation of everyday life such as sharing a meal, shopping, participating in your work environment, hiking a trail, whale watching, gardening, or any other activity. Imagine each participant as existing in the microtonal space between the activity of the moment and you. The activity becomes the story with each participant coloring the space between the story and other. Imagine stories as connectors, filling the spaces between moments. The spaces hold the emotional content of our stories. They are the microtonal resonators of life.

THE SPACE
BETWEEN

The microtonal space is more than a space between tones. The space between is a window of opportunity in which the flexibility to create change and transformation exists. The heart of microtonal healing beats in the space between. The space opens to Great Mystery, a sacred place of infinite potential and healing energy. It can be compared to absolute zero, referred to in quantum physics, which is full of energy. The sacred space or void even exists in our cells (Capra 1980; Leonard 1981). It is a universe with which we are intimately acquainted, yet its multifaceted role in the flow of life and the healing process remains to be consciously acknowledged and explored.

In a culture that is focused on outcome and grandeur, the microspaces in daily life are something we tend to ignore. They become insignificant, even invisible. Imagine flipping a light switch on or off. There are expectations prompted by an unconscious assumption that light will be turned on or off. The point in between on and off, where light is coming into being or being extinguished, is minuscule. The potentiality of both light and dark exist in the space. It is those micropoints between the initiation of action and outcome that are the substance of life. They are essential to the process of living.

Life is in a perpetual state of transition. We move in and out of balance whether we are aware of the movement or not. This movement is prompted by the continual emotional fluctuations of living experience. Because the movement is so infinitesimal, the transitional activity occurring in the microtonal space is not always apparent and does not enter cognitive awareness. However, any movement is always perceived by somatic consciousness within every cell and atom of the body.

Developing a conscious relationship with the power of the microtonal space as a place of renewal and healing begins with microtonal singing. The quality of attention and focus that is awakened with microtonal singing sensitizes awareness to take notice of microshifts from moment to moment. They cannot be vocally ignored because microtonal singing prompts acknowledgment of micro sounds and movements in daily life. Through increasing conscious awareness of micromovements in every aspect of being, attention can be given to maintaining balance.

You might begin to notice that life patterns have ups and downs that periodically open to silent and empty spaces, unpredictable moments. They are spaces in which to retreat and be still. They provide for periods of incubation where Great Mystery is at play in the realm of possibilities. There are times in the transitional process when it is appropriate to linger in the mystery of the microtonal space. You might feel as if all action is frozen in time because movement is not apparent in the visible world. It can be likened to being caught in the middle of a sruti between notes. The space between is nebulous, pliable, shifting, unrestrictive in its vastness, open to possibilities and creative potential free from judgment. Microtones reflect life experiences as they quaver, slide up and down, and are punctuated by silent spaces. Being in a microtonal space can feel chaotic, as if something within needs to be set free. It can also feel desperately empty, as if something within is screaming out to be filled. Either way, the microtonal space is a gateway to the next place.

A process of transition is underway in the microtonal space. It can be a place of calm or one in which anxiety takes hold. When perceived as the unknown, the microtonal space can incite a sense of discomfort, indecision, or even depression. The unknown, more often than not, is something we are taught to fear. When fear shadows consciousness in the void of the space, it can feel as if the safety and stability to which we want to cling has dropped away. There can be a sense of isolation and aloneness, sometimes described as the dark night of the soul, as if connection to Spirit is lost.

Yet this is only the appearance of separation because the visible and invisible realms are connected by the space between. The space between does not separate you from the Source, it places you nearer to Spirit. The space unites you with the wisdom of infinite blessings, particularly during a time of transition. That is when you have a foot in both worlds. That is when you stand on shifting sands in a realm of infinite possibilities and creative ideas. The space between is where microtonal shifts occur to maintain balance in the transitional process from one state to another. For that reason, the microtonal space can feel unstable. The instability is transitional and momentary until a firm footing is restored.

When you find yourself in the void of a space in the flow of life, stop. Remember that the void is within. As you fear the void and the emptiness, so you fear the internal place where transformation lives. Instead, think of yourself as being in the heart of Great Mystery, in the presence of Divine Guidance. Trust that micromovements are at play and are guided by the spiritual aspects of being, the all-knowing wisdom of Higher Consciousness. It can become a journey into the far reaches of a star-studded night sky, each star illuminating your awareness with the wonder of expanding consciousness.

Consciously living in the mystery of the unknown from moment to moment requires trust and an act of faith as you leap from the illusory tower of knowing. Cherish the unknown as a natural place of being rather than as a place of waiting. Explore microtonal spaces by delving into meditation between concepts and images. Take time to notice the point between sound and silence, between movement and stillness, between one thought and the next, between sleep and awake, and between doing and not doing. For example, imagine a microspace between the yin and yang of the Tao symbol, between the light and the dark.

Allow yourself to enter the space by mentally situating yourself so that you sense light on one side and dark on the other. From within the space between light and dark, you can perceive the qualities of each—one at a time at first, then simultaneously. In doing so, you become poised at the center of your being. There you will find images of wholeness and a sense of being embraced by the Source. The ability to focus awakens as you are graced with an awareness of the now. Intuitive wisdom springs to life revealing broad vision in the heart of stillness. Loving compassion for life, for ourselves, and for others is awakened and judgment is naturally suspended.

Judgment occurs from opposite poles in which the health and beauty of diversity in life is invisible. Polarities exist in relationships of opposites, such as sound and silence, movement and stillness, good and bad, and left and right. Both polarities are necessary in relational balance. Neither is right or wrong. One is necessary to the other. We are often caught in polarities when we have to make decisions. In the microtonal space between each polarity or duality, there is a point of awareness in which judgment falls by the wayside. In the absence of judgment, the value of each polarity can be appreciated. New options then spring to light allowing for actions and words that neither offend nor discredit.

Awareness unfolds into pure observation when we enter the space between. As pure observation comes to the fore, opposites flow into each other, each laughing with the other. They are mutually inclusive. It prompts a delightful awakening when we embrace diversity in this manner and recognize it as natural in the oneness of life. We need to cultivate and cherish more of this type of awareness in our lives, in our families, in our communities, in our nation, in our world.

As a point of observation, the microtonal space is a place of great awareness, awakening strands of consciousness and retrieving them from an ocean of possibilities and probable realities. It can be likened to standing in the stillness between currents. It is a point of clarity from which to experience an energetic force, a swirling power. It is an opportunity to witness chaos and order in an exchange of energy and information. Nothing is fixed in the space between. It is the edge between chaos and order. It is an area of transition. Yet the microtonal space is a still point in the Great Mystery.

Working with sound opens us to new dimensions of listening to the silence between sounds. Being attentive to the space between words, for example, prompts a different kind of focus. We always hear the silence in sound or there would be no cadence to speech. There would be no rhythm in song or in life sounds. However, the spaces between words hold emotional content. That is what touches us when we are engaged in conversation.

As an exercise to develop an awareness of the effect of silent spaces on consciousness, listen to the beat of a metronome set at about sixty beats per minute. Listen to the spaces between the beat and gradually reduce the rhythmic rate. Continue listening to the space between beats as the rhythm slows. Notice the mental shift. Gradually increase the beat of the metronome. Again, notice the shift in consciousness.

Catch the space between the ticks of a clock. Listen to the untick. The tick of the clock fades as the space in between ticks captures the attention. You will come to realize that movement resides in the space. It is the space that pushes the hands of the clock forward. When the ticking stops, all returns to a point of stillness, a silent space so vast it contains all motion and sound. It is conceivable that the silent space between sound and the still point between breaths are doorways to other realms.

Pay attention to your response to silent spaces when they occur in your life. Develop an awareness of what silence holds for you by taking time to slow down. As part of your daily vocal healing practice, enter the silence for at least two minutes. Be in the space and observe how you relate to silence emotionally, physically, spiritually, and mentally. Then sound again. When you complete your practice session, welcome the invitation of silence for another brief period.

Silence is a part of living. Silence can be seen to occupy a space between events. In time, you will begin to experience silence as a necessary resting place. The silence can induce a transcendent state in which you are poised in the moment and open to gathering your energy to effortlessly regain mental focus and clarity. Simply be in the silence. Everything takes care of itself. Whatever you need hovers in the wings of silence gently gracing you with its presence. You will find magic in the silence as your own natural rhythm of life unfolds.

Cultivating the silent space between tones stimulates a meditative deepening. It is part of the microtonal process. Emotional awareness deepens as you come to appreciate the quiet spaces. It is in the depths that you will find your roots, your source of strength and stability. They are roots that nourish as they tap into the heart of life on earth. It is only through experiencing the depths that the ability to soar to the heights of Spirit develops. The silence thus opens to a sacred place of grace where you can embrace the All with an open heart.

Silence becomes a path for consciousness to delve into the depths of Great Mystery. It is an empty space and yet it is the container of all. The space is silent and still. As a silent space, it holds sound; as a still place, it holds movement. Imagine a silent satin sack that contains sound. When the silent sack is turned inside out, sound becomes the container of silence. In the silence, sound incubates until it spills forth and envelops the silence. Silence and sound are alive. Notice the silence. Notice the sound. Notice how each opens into the other. Focus your attention on the promise of life incubating in the still silence.

The microtonal space is alive, expanding and contracting in a rhythmic breath of relationship with life. As a momentary flicker in the flow of life, the sacred space is a passageway through which sound can be entered in its living, pulsating fullness. Recognize the space as a place of potential that awaits vocal summons to stimulate insight and healing. Relish the mystery of the unknown as if it were a luxurious and velvety-soft night sky studded with microtonal stars waiting to be sung. Bathe the unknown with shimmering strands of light by singing the microtones that arise from the mystery of the space. Great Mystery is given tonal form by singing the space. The colorful threads of light that abound in the unknown then ride on your voice in vibrational waves to restore resonance and a sense of well-being.

We experience a multitude of microtonal spaces in the course of a lifetime. They are opportunities to examine the world from a new perspective. It is in the space where the substance of life will be found. The microspaces in life add texture and meaning. The spaces between action, between sound, and between events deserve attention. They are the glue between events that are meant to be experienced and enjoyed. The spaces give life cohesiveness because they are the energetic link holding it all together.

Ours is a culture that is geared toward action. We are taught to keep busy. If we stop for a moment, silence and stillness can press in and demand attention. Those are moments when we turn on the television to fill the silence. Our environment then becomes flooded with horrific events as the media reports the worst and most sensational news of the day. The so-called entertainment that follows is commonly filled with violent and unpleasant images. Unconsciously, we hold our breath, not daring to feel anything.

Opening to the gifts of silence must be a conscious act in the beginning in order to reprogram years of training to fear the emptiness of a silent and still space. Fear has been associated with the stillness before an earthquake or the calm before a storm. We are conditioned to think the worst. However, it is also quiet before the birds begin singing in the morning. Black and white thinking has no place in microtonal consciousness. Microtones are too full of color. There are always other options awaiting recognition from the space between.

How many silent spaces do we jump over like some great chasm to be avoided in the course of a day? They are there. They pass unnoticed because they are not permitted in the psyche of modern life. The psyche longs to hang out in moments of silence, stillness, and calm, yet we have to consciously allow awareness of the calm to unfold. Take a moment to remember the space of calm and reclaim your center. Breathe in deeply, fully aware that the silent space is an opportunity to connect with your soul essence.

As the vessel and conveyor of pure emotional energy, the microtonal space is a place of healing transition. Singing the space microtonally stirs the emotions. It methodically nurtures the heart in the moment, making it a conscious process. Always in the moment and always going deeper. By going deeply into the microtonal space with your voice, you are cultivating the soil in your emotional garden. Loosen the emotional earth with your microtonal voice to allow tender shoots of healing wisdom to sprout from within the space. Then notice a state of well-being growing into a feeling of wholeness and contentment in who you are.

HIGHER FREQUENCIES

The microtonal space and the effect of vibrational frequencies on that space are key to understanding microtonal healing concepts. When observing the effect of vibrational frequencies on matter, such as that presented in the work of Hans Jenny (1974, 1986), we notice that higher vibrational frequencies create intricate patterns. Matter vibrates into refined threadlike filaments, becoming almost translucent strands in response to higher frequencies of sound. Space increases in the pattern as matter is refined. Applying this phenomenon to human frequencies of bodymind, it is conceivable that as you increase your vibrational frequency, more room is psychically available within which to move and explore.

Slower brainwave patterns permit us to merge consciousness with the electromagnetic field of higher and finer frequencies. It seems contradictory to say that the slower brain wave patterns transport consciousness to dimensions of higher frequencies. That is a paradox of the slower alpha and theta brainwaves that produce meditative states and allow transcendence into a field of higher and finer vibrations. By slowing down into a state of calm relaxation in which you can more easily focus, you are able to slip through spaces to other dimensions. Three-dimensional reality appears to slow down. There is more space in which to be and to appreciate each breath of vital energy when you are consciously poised in the moment.

Time and space go hand in hand in our three-dimensional world. When perceived in the light of a space time continuum, as space increases at higher frequencies, time expands. More space and time in which to live consciously come into being as space time is experienced as expanding. Because the higher vibrations are less dense, there is more space between strands of consciousness in the invisible realm. Mental clarity and focus replace confusion. A sense of order comes into play. Imagine strands of consciousness as threadlike filaments of light and color emanating from your soul essence. The life force can flow freely when the colorful light strands become untangled and can breathe.

When living within higher vibrations of heightened awareness, spiritual dimensions become available. The ability to accomplish more in the same amount of clock time occurs. It might feel as if you are slowing down, yet you are simply functioning optimally in earth time. You move purposefully as your vibrational rate increases and the material world maintains its same rate of vibration. You are not caught off guard. A microtonal space at higher frequencies is optimum for decision making because of the expanded awareness of choices. Strands of consciousness that offer choices spring into light. You are able to take in more information, evaluate that information, and act upon it with more accuracy and decisiveness. Flexibility in exercising options that are beneficial gives new freedom to life. With it comes a knowingness that there is no need to hurry. There is room for everything that needs to be accomplished.

Lower vibrational frequencies reduce our experience of time and space. The space contracts. Energy becomes chaotic and jumbled as threads of consciousness become tangled in a confined space. The ability to focus bumps into itself. Visual, auditory, emotional, mental, and physical disorientation results. The tendency to jump from one activity to another in the fast pace of daily life prevails and does not lend itself to flowing with the shifting rhythms of natural order. When you sense space time contracting into a blurred field of clutter, allow yourself to slow down by singing the space.

A heightened state of awareness in the moment is cultivated with vocal meditation practices, particularly with microtonal singing. Being in tune and emanating higher vibrations of light and love allow you to live at the center of expanded space time. Being poised in the center, in the space of unlimited potential, relaxation increases and greater precision in action allows more to be accomplished. Microtonal singing helps you locate and access that space to optimum advantage in daily life. Luxuriate in the space. Amid the space in higher frequencies, consciousness is free to expand and to fully experience the moment in a state of readiness.

Creativity abounds within higher vibrational frequencies as possibilities for change increase. More choices of notes to sing into life become available. While it is impossible to grasp all possibilities at once, you can sort and choose the threads of consciousness on which to focus in the expanded microtonal space. You might find your entire life changing direction as awareness clicks in. Suddenly, you know what you need to do to follow your path, to allow your essence to shine. It sounds idyllic, yet it occurs as a natural flow of life when you access higher vibrations from the microtonal space.

The space within higher frequencies is one of expanded awareness in time, a healing place where there is more room for emotional awareness and insights. Refined strands of emotional energy are lighter and make way for mental clarity. Microtones live in the spaces. The higher the vibration the greater the space for microtones to come into play and dance in the rhythmic flow of life.

As higher frequencies increase the space, awareness of emotions is likely to increase as well. Order occurs at higher frequencies, however, and emotions fall into place or become integrated into consciousness. This could account for more resolution with microtonal singing as a healing practice.

The microtonal voice modulates the slightest nuance of emotional energy into alignment, thereby creating coherent patterns in the electromagnetic field.

Emotions carry the impetus to create transformation. When desire flows from the heart of your soul essence, it is empowered by the higher frequencies of love and joy. The joy of living from the heart and in a state of balance thus becomes accessible.

THE MICROTONAL
FLOW OF LIFE

Microtonal flow is best defined as the dance of life that opens to the heart and the pleasure of being alive. The very nature of microtones gives rise to the concept of the microtonal flow of life. Microtones unfold in the singing as luminous threads of pulsating vocal energy that catch our attention. Poised to change direction as they flutter on the breath, microtones flow effortlessly with the mood and color of the moment. The tones present themselves, unfurling their unique attributes of being elusive and playful. Microtones can dive to the depths of being and soar to spiritual heights by allowing the voice to slide up and down or to flutter and fly in the emotional spaces between stable tones. They can also disappear into the silence as mysteriously as they arose.

The unpredictable manner in which microtones arise from the space between notes reflects the continuous flow of events rippling through our lives. Life is unrehearsed, and microtonal singing is always improvisational and spontaneous. Even within a melodic pattern, with the voice flickering in and out of stability, no note can follow predictably. The singer might begin as if a melodic plan is in place, when in reality there is no plan other than trusting the wisdom of the voice to flow with emotional integrity in the moment. The microtonal voice embraces the substance of life by revealing the emotional energy of the place and time. It supports awareness of the life-affirming melodies in our lives.

Change and unpredictability pulsate throughout our lives, a process of starts and stops that creates patterns and textures in rhythmic waves. Developing awareness of rhythmic patterns in life is an integral part of microtonal healing. The microtonal voice undulates in rhythm with the flow of life. It develops an ability within the singer to flow with and respond to the unexpected, those places of change that both conceal and reveal the unknown in a spiraling and undulating cycle of life. Nothing is fixed or predetermined, but rather than feeling out of control, we are challenged to surf vocal waves in the moment, fully prepared for any shifts that might occur. We are challenged to increase awareness of how we flow in the process of living. We are engaged in a vibrational dance within ourselves and with the energy around us. Microtonal singing provides an opportunity to learn the dance of life while consciously riding the waves of change that occur in daily living. We learn to shift and flow first with the singing voice and then to apply the principles to daily life.

Microtonal flow reveals a natural and continual process of transformation. The microtonal voice illuminates this natural fluidity of life as a conscious adventure. The fluidity of the microtonal voice invites us to appreciate that everything is in a state of flux, always moving toward a state of grace and balance. The voice finds its way, weaving a path between movement and stability. Movement and stillness flow one into the other. Stability is momentary. Flux is momentary. Each is present in the other. Flux is the nature of life and is therefore life's stability. Being is not static. Being ripples and flows, swirls and churns, and becoming silent here and there, it pauses to appreciate the movement in stillness. As we learn to flow with the perpetual motion and shifting that is inherent in life, we can coordinate and appreciate a life of balance in the flux with the microtonal voice as a guide.

Life is a maze that changes with each step and each step holds the potential to change the maze. Flowing with the moment means living consciously, moving with awareness, and being prepared to respond to any circumstance. Alert to the unpredictability of the natural flow at every turn, the ability to live without expectation in what can only be experienced as sweet abandon takes hold. You can stop momentarily to deepen your experience of a place. A silence might be inserted when it is prompted by a fleeting impulse to be still. An emotion might be calling the singer to go deeper by eliciting quavering microtones. An integrity of being and personhood is sustained while permitting depth of exploration.

Diving to the depths of being reveals random twists and turns that form intricate life patterns. The twists and turns and switchback trails of life are opportunities of discovery and creative potential. They are important pieces of the journey that add perspective and give life meaning and hope. Notice whether you try skipping over them in an effort to take the fastest and most direct route to achieving a goal or arriving at a destination. The destination can be mistaken as an end, but an end does not exist. What is perceived as an end is a momentary point of balance, seeming stability that shifts and changes in the journey of life. It is part of the never-ending process of transformation. The destination or end might better be described as a point that is awaiting discovery within a microtonal space.

In reality, the only destination in life is to be in the moment and to appreciate variation of the landscape. To do that, it is necessary to slow down, notice the shifts, and to step with awareness. Living within the flexibility of the microtonal flow, spontaneous and intuitive decision-making processes direct action or inaction with focus and intent. A conscious shifting of gears and perspective takes hold as a new beginning falls into place. After a while, focused abandon in living becomes a conscious way of life in a universe of flux.

Consider the nooks and crannies of Victorian houses as exhibiting microtonal characteristics. They add a charm that is missing from stark square or rectangular rooms by contributing to the essence of the place. They reveal bits and pieces about the people who have adorned those spaces with emotional artifacts that hold reminiscences. Such treasures become as sacred objects that offer moments of nurturing and well-being to those who imbue them with meaning. Icons of time rise up in their special nooks catching the emotions of those who behold them, just as srutis rise up from an inconspicuous microtonal space quavering on the breath. They represent emotional moments in life and offer access to rich memories in folds of time. The verbally inexpressible is contained in the object, and the object says it all. That is the function of microtones as well. They convey deep emotional meaning without words.

The microtonal space embraces the essence of being, your soul essence. From that place, you can touch Spirit. It is a transitional realm. It is part of the microtonal flow of life, the ups and downs, the ebb and flow. As with microtones, we dip in and out of silent spaces. Those moments can feel as if you are caught in the middle of a sruti, that microtonal space of flux between notes. You can experience the depth and height, the emptiness and fullness, all at once. When you find yourself in a microtonal space, it is a sign to slow down, to reflect on who you are deep within. Take pause for a brief period from the busi-ness of the day. Give yourself a moment to reflect on where you are and what it means to be in the space between.

Experiencing a time of emotional overload or depletion can feel as if you have stepped into a dark hole, a void, not unlike the microtonal space. At those times, the emotions are flat, the mind is dull, the body is weary, and it seems as if Spirit hovers somewhere in the shadows. You might feel as if you have moved farther away from a comfort zone and that something you relied on for security and balance in your life has fallen away. A comfort zone isn't necessarily a place of balance. Often a comfort zone is only a place of seeming equilibrium that has become habitual and familiar.

During times of change in the cycle of life, you will not be shifting back again to the old ways of being. This realiza-tion can bring a sense of relief as well as sadness. The psyche is filled with a sense of instability while also trying desperate-ly to connect with something solid and tangible, something familiar. Acknowledge and honor your sense of loss at leav-ing the familiar behind when this occurs. It is natural to expe-rience a grieving process. Consciously trusting the presence of connection to Spirit in times of change and transformation can take courage, a leap of faith that ultimately leads to a new sense of freedom. Microtonal singing helps in this process as the srutis modulate any emotional rough edges with their undulating and quavering nature. Imagine balance being restored to every space in every atom and with it comes a more flexible and balanced footing in the world. We are always guided when we allow the breath of Spirit to direct our microtonal voice.

Remember that srutis live between the stability of svaras or stable notes. Creativity abounds in the space of the sruti and makes way for transition to stability. Although you might feel as if you are floundering in the depths of a space, fluttering is part of the healing process. The microtonal voice honors the movement between flux and flow, and chaos and order. Fear of the unknown dissipates as order flows out of chaos. It is as if srutis are aware of an order in the chaos. They know how to dance in a clear flutter of tones.

As much as we might like to say it isn't so, we do live in a chaotic universe. The microtonal space is integral to the flow of life. Stability will return as will the microtonal space of flux so we might as well be prepared to acknowledge and enjoy the presence of both. They are just a microtonal movement away from each other. Perceiving the flow of life in this manner can be an awakening. The more we become sensitized to micromovements in our lives, the easier it is to maintain balance, and the easier it is to delight in the gifts of this dance of life. Microtonal singing shows us that chaos and order are apparent from the microtonal space and yields to the concept of the microtonal flow as a process. Microtonal healing processes bring that reality to conscious awareness, and the microtonal voice allows us to enjoy it.

Microtonal singing teaches us to pay attention to the intuitive knowing that is always available. The space comes alive in the microtonal musical structure. Release your hold on seeming stability and enjoy the undulating joy of the microtonal space. Trust that you are moving forward into a new and balanced order. A solid footing will be restored and, without realizing it, you will become stable as a svara with a sense of well-being once again. The place of the svara helps to put things into perspective. Order is restored and with it comes clarity.

We want assurances that we know what the future will bring; however, we live in the mystery. At the same time, we ignore the mystery and seek shelter from the unknown. With microtonal singing, we can seek to know and embrace the gifts of power and light within the Great Mystery. Acknowledging the microtonal space is to acknowledge the mystery in the landscape of life, the potential for change as well as the bridges that enable change. We are creative beings with limitless potential and endless possibilities. We are creating paths and bridges all the time, and microtonal processes challenge us to risk dreaming new possibilities. The space is multidimensional, a point between the visible and invisible realms. It is our connection to Spirit, to All That Is. The microtonal space is an opening through which pure consciousness travels when we dare to dream and to go with the flow.

THE MICROTONAL NATURE
OF OUR ENVIRONMENT

Microtonal singing instills a deep appreciation of nature. It awakens sensory perception of that which is innate in us, the ability to resonate with nature because we are a part of nature. The invisible and inaudible aspects of our organic environment are enlivened with the microtonal voice as it establishes an energetic connection with the living earth. Nature is in tune, and by joining with her in microtonal splendor, a state of resonant balance is renewed within our being.

When we relax into nature, the emotional space opens and we are one with all of life. Have you ever rested beneath the shade of an ancient oak tree, in an old-growth forest, or in a meadow garden where harmony and beauty caress the stillness? They become spaces in which to slow down and listen with our being. Nature reveals its resonance to the senses. Environmental awareness expands as every aspect of nature whispers its presence, offering assurance that we exist as one in the web of life.

The song of nature is composed of harmonic diversity. Diversity is essential to the texture and health of life, for it is the luminous threads of diversity that constitute the web of life. As species are being destroyed, as languages are being forgotten, our planet loses another melody, another song, another rhythmic presence that plays a part in holding life in balance. To develop and emit our own vocal sounds, which have been silenced, is to restore awareness of the beauty and creative energy that abounds within us and within every cell and atom of every living thing. As we learn to explore microtonal awareness and to treasure our own songs and laughter, doors of tolerance open. Systems of harmonic diversity are embraced.

Take microtonal singing on hikes in nature. Listen to nature's subtle sounds and soft whispers. Listen to the fullness of life sounds, their texture, shape, and color. Open to perceive the microtonality of life and allow it to become a musical extension of your physical presence. Microtones sung playfully connect us with the spiritual energy of earth, teaching us to listen for the melody of life with all of its luxurious tones and rhythms. Your experience will be one of merging with the natural environment. Listening to the sounds of nature can become a meditation practice in which personal attunement with nature is developed. It nurtures a realization that we are a part of every speck of life. There is no limit to our spiritual nature except what we put there.

Singing with nature in your garden, an atrium, a meadow, a forest, beside a waterfall, the ocean, or a river cultivates heightened awareness of the natural environment. Listen to the spaces in your environment for they are filled with melodies of the web of life. Sing the spaces while reflecting on your voice and join with the vibrational energy of your natural environment. You will come to recognize that higher vibrations exist in resonance with nature.

Microtonal singing embellishes the beauty of the tonal landscape. Like nature, the microtonal voice has texture, shape, and color. Practice entering into the fullness of your vocal tones. Step into the sound of your voice. Experience its living qualities. Then you can sing the totality of the landscape. Sing a blossoming flower in short, tonal bursts or full and resonant tones. Sing along with a cricket's chirp or the whirring drone of a hummingbird's wings. Listen for the microtonal melodies of robins, warblers, and sparrows. Join in with your microtonal voice. As we sing with the earth, we consciously sing with life, renewing the earth, our bodies, minds, and spirits. It is a reminder of the oneness of life.

Notice the currents and back flows in river rapids and streams exhibiting a microtonal flavor. Sing that rippling and undulating movement with microtonal fluttering and sliding. Let your voice follow the fluidity and currents of the river for a while. You might begin singing as if in harmony with the river's flow. Then listen to your internal rhythm and let your voice express the patterns of your unique microtonal flow. It is sometimes easier to let your voice lead. Your voice flows from the body and is intimately acquainted with your internal rhythm. Listen to its wisdom as it plays your rhythmic microtonal dance. At the same time, notice the flow and currents of the river. Notice where you meet the river's flow and harmonize or where you diverge on a different course. Notice when you go deeper, perhaps by entering the silence. Exercises such as this awaken consciousness to your role in the symphony of life.

A walk in the woods, along the beach, or anywhere in nature will provide a less structured climate for singing microtonally. It will instill in you a sense of free-flowing flexibility as you sing. Your singing can become imbued with a playfulness as you fall into rhythm with the hills and valleys of the landscape. It is not unusual for tones to bend with the landscape, rising to reflect walking uphill and falling while on the downhill slope of a trail. Flexibility can be reinforced in consciousness from such a seemingly simple observation.

Microtonal singing can transport a person into an altered state of consciousness, and it also instills a sense of physical presence within the environment. Playing with your voice energetically develops a sonic bodily awareness in which the environment comes alive with vibrational energy. Become involved with the sound of your voice. Focus your attention on the feeling of vocalizing within your body. Receive your voice tones with your ears, through your skin, and in every cell and atom. Receive the vibrations of your voice tones into your bones. Pay attention to where a tone or flutter is felt in your body. Notice the energetic quality of your vocal tones in every aspect of your being. Consciously interact with microtones to develop a sonic physical awareness within yourself, and between yourself and your natural environment.

Let your favorite song become the sound of your voice singing tones and microtones with nature. Listen to the microtonal notes of your internal improvisational tune as tonal memory within the body is called into play. Listen to your environment with your external ears while embracing the melody internally. Let the sound of leaves crunching beneath your feet catch your attention as you walk through a park or along a trail. Link these sounds with the chattering of blue jays or the call of a hawk and notice the natural intertwining of melody and rhythm. Listening to nature as a meditation practice evolves over time. As you cultivate awareness of your inner sound, you will recognize that music is playing on the inside while music is playing around you in the sounds of nature. Allow yourself to hear the earth so that you can sing with her.

In the silence that follows singing, take time to slow down and listen. In the silence, every cell and atom of your physical body listens. Listen to your body listening and you will come to recognize silence as a sacred space within. This sacred space is a passageway through which sound is entered in its living, pulsating fullness. Breathe in the sound of silence. Breathe in the moment. With each breath, you are involved in an exchange of energy and consciousness with your environment.

The microtonal voice can also be related to the motion of the tide. We can join the dance of life in step with its rhythmic ebb and flow. The ebbing tide demonstrates how to recede in order to regain a sense of balance. The microtonal space is a place in which to do that as well. It is a place to consciously reflect, to shift and adjust before proceeding. Relaxing into vocal fluttering when the flow of life ebbs supports that process. We need to remember this when we find ourselves in a slump or experiencing depression.

When the tide flows inward, it connects more fully with the shore like microtones connecting with the stable svaras. The incoming tide deposits secrets of the deep to be revealed when the ebb cycles out again. Resistance to sinking to the depths is a natural reaction. Standing barefoot in the receding flow of an ocean wave, you might notice your toes digging into the sand to brace yourself against the undercurrent. The tendency is to cling to that which is stable. Psychologically, resistance to sinking into the depths stems from fear of the darkness and of facing the shadow. Becoming mindful that the microtonal voice arises from the depths of the space where creativity abounds helps in overcoming such fearful resistance. The ebb reveals treasures nurtured in the depths, in the space. Taking time to retreat with the ebb, to sing the space, and to become acquainted with its treasures nourishes the soul. It enables us to catch the wave and enjoy the ride when the tide flows in again.

Microtones teach us about patterns of nature that are forever coming into being and going out of being. Microtones nestle between stability, supporting movement and serving as a reminder to play and explore the dance of life with sweet abandon. Remember that the earth is round. As it turns and we step forward, there is a place to catch the footfall. Then again, there might be a space needing to be filled with a microtonal adventure. It is natural to live in the unknown. We only assume predictability in the next moment. That is what allows us to sidestep any thought of the unknown and to live with hope and assurance that all is well. That is human nature and also the nature of human folly.

A microtonal space cannot be revisited. Not only is it a new space, but microtones become weary of a repetitive tune. Movement is inherent in microtones. They quaver improvisationally. The microtonal voice wanders in undulating curves and rhythms reflecting emotional themes in a process that mirrors ever-changing spirals of energy. Spirals can move up or down, in or out, forward or backward, ever cycling in expanding and contracting movement. A spiral is the natural movement of life processes. There is always movement and change along a spiral path, and there is always transformation with microtonal practices. Predictability and unchanging stability in life are not possible. Microtones will not allow it. Neither will nature. The adventure of life would be lost.

If a grain of sand moves back and forth in the same place over a period of time, everything around it is altered with each movement. Through seemingly repetitive movement, microtonal shifts occur. Movement of any kind cannot be repeated precisely. Our experience of the world is altered even with seeming repetition. As experience is altered, repetition dissolves. The experience is new. The shifts are barely perceptible to the senses until you slow down. In developing an understanding of microtonal processes, you come to realize that repetition without change is an illusion because repetition becomes unconscious action that dulls the senses to change. Repetition is never precise because it is not possible.

Repetition is best perceived as a renewal of what preceded it, as a spiraling activity. As with the cycle of seasons, every season is transformed by the seasons that precede and follow it. Nothing about nature is repetitious. Seasons and cycles bring change. Each season unfolds anew. Each spring offers budding new life. The warmth and vibrance of summer swells the earth to maturity. With fall comes another harvest, a different harvest. Winter reveals crisp sounds and night skies studded with stars more dazzling than the heart remembers. The earth reveals its creativity in ever-increasing abundance through its joyful and magnificent dance of life. There is no actual and precise repetition. What is described as repetition always begins fresh in a new moment, arising from a distinct point in time.

Repetition transforms while creating an illusion of sameness. You can draw a circle on top of a circle without altering its size or shape, but what has gone before will shine through and what follows is an entirely new circle. If you continue with the circular motion, it will eventually develop a blip in it somewhere and begin to spiral, usually outward, which is an indication of blossoming and growth. Every repetitive action is unique. It can be no other way because we live in time and space.

Fractals provide another example of nonrepetition. With fractals, twists and turns are generated through bifurcation, a natural process of splitting in random directions. A similar process is exhibited in microtonal singing as the voice flows along for a time and then pauses, quavers, or changes direction. Nature displays a bifurcation process in the formation of branches and leaves on plants and trees. Patterns develop through a natural process of growth, yet every flower and plant is unique unto itself. This is so for every life form and for each person. We live in the midst of natural perfection and we are a part of it.

In geometry, fractals evolve into patterns in the form of Mandelbrot sets, which would appear to contradict the nonrepetitive notion. Mandelbrot sets are paisley-like images that upon magnification, reveal an infinite replication of fractal patterns. However, the fractals arise randomly within a shifting context of relational placement. As one small section of the image is enlarged, the details of the pattern are seen to be replicated in the process of bifurcation. As in nature, there is diversion that ultimately gives way to patterns. The location of the fractal and therefore its context are altered as it assumes a place in intricate and ever-evolving sets and patterns. Moving beyond seeming repetition, an undulating landscape unfolds.

Repetition is a process. Even if we become stuck for a time, it is part of the process. For example, retracing a circle or a pattern in sand will create an increasingly deeper path.

When we walk a path enough times, our presence begins to alter it. We leave a print, a mark. As we continue retracing our steps, change escapes awareness and the path becomes a rut. The rut takes us deeper without our even realizing it. It can be thought of as a path that has forgotten how to spiral in more than one direction. Every repetition creates change. We are always moving on to new notes, but sometimes we need to do it consciously to change direction. Microtonal singing helps us do that.

The rhythm of life in nature reveals points of stillness between sound, between movement, between seasons. It is points of stillness and silence that produce rhythmic patterns. Microtonal singing teaches us to stop periodically and enter the still point of silence. It is the space in which access to higher frequencies is available. Higher frequencies expand the space in which we experience life. In the expanded space of higher frequencies, love has room to grow and fill our lives. Time also expands, allowing us to slow down and luxuriate in life's rhythm with a full and open heart.

Most of us are taught from the moment of birth that we are separate from nature. Separation from and dominance over anything that is not human is deeply embedded in the western psyche. Removed from nature and affected by artificial environments at every turn, the natural tonality of being is altered. The state of perfect resonance and rhythm that most people have at birth becomes lost within the lower frequencies of a mechanistic environment. The microtonal spaces that hold life together are smaller amid lower frequencies and time is compacted. The time and space for emotionality decreases because emotions inhabit the microtonal space. Even love becomes pushed into a tiny space, diminishing its presence in our lives. The pace quickens into a frenzy. Rapid shifts push and pull physically, mentally, emotionally. Attention and focus become scattered, which could be an explanation for more attention deficit disorder diagnoses in recent years.

American culture is focused principally on visual stimuli. With television and videos being introduced at such an early age, children are visually overstimulated and learn to perceive life at a distance, unattached. It is a desensitization process that dulls the senses with collage images flashing on the television screen. The ability to focus and sustain attention flies between images. It is not possible to take in anything deeply and consciously given the pace of visual bombardment presented to us through the media, especially television. The fast-paced flashing of visual images could be a contributing factor to an onslaught of mental and physical overwhelm. Viewing repeated, rapidly flashing lights can also stimulate the occurrence of seizures.

In addition, we are bombarded with intrusive sounds in our daily environments. As a result, we tune out sound to such an extent that we have become unaware of its impact on our well-being. Not only do we tune out environmental sounds, we no longer listen to our internal sounds. Because we no longer listen, we have lost our sense of being both in tune and out of tune.

Listening as a spiritual practice expands and deepens life experiences. Through listening with your whole being to the sounds and textures of your voice, environmental sounds begin to take on a new quality. Annoyance at otherwise intrusive environmental sounds dissipates as you learn to exist in relationship with them. Some environmental sounds support and complement the voice in the same way that a drone provides support for microtones within a melodic raga. Even the sounds of a leaf blower outside the window or an airplane passing overhead can be enjoyed as drone harmony to support the microtonal voice. They can be acknowledged as the sruti boxes of technology rather than as intrusions into your microtonal singing space.

Microtonal singing lightens the spirit by heightening sensory awareness on every level. It acquaints us with the space between and dissolves the illusion of separation from Spirit, from the environment and from one another. We begin to understand that when we deny nature, we deny our creaturehood, our inner substance and our connection to life. The energy field of the human body, perceived as the aura, is continuous. It blends with the electromagnetic field in a flowing exchange of energy with everyone and everything in our environment. This is particularly relevant with regard to the transmission of healing energy. As we bring ourselves into a state of well-being, the natural environment is healed as well. As we heal ourselves, we heal all of life on earth and beyond.

Microtonal singing follows the course of nature, which is in a constant state of change. It brings the natural flow and rhythm of life to the light of awareness. Flux is the dance of life and we are a part of it. Microtonal singing reflects that dance, the unpredictable adventure of life so abundant and bold in nature. Even those new to the practice of microtonal singing feel as if they have stepped through a musical opening into the shimmering substance of life that arises unpredictably from the wellspring of Great Mystery. Perhaps that will be your experience, too.

MICROTONAL MOVEMENT

Microtonal movement is a product of microtonal singing. However, they are independent practices. The microtonal voice teaches us about the microtonality of transformational processes. Microtonal movement is an application of that teaching that allows us to take that awareness to another level of experience.

The principal purpose of microtonal movement is to become conscious of the smallest movements within the body. It is a practice designed to induce relaxation and focus while increasing flexibility without stress or strain. You can feel a comfortable and gradual extension of your muscles that results from release through relaxation. Whether you are stiff mentally or physically, you can enjoy an easy stretching and alignment of bodymind. Make an agreement with your Self to pay attention to micromovements as part of your daily microtonal practice.

If you have become stiff due to lack of exercise, the small movements are a first step toward developing the physical flexibility that you once enjoyed. Your commitment to microtonal consciousness is ending a phase of existence that is ready for change. It is also your commitment to beginning a new way of being in the world. Listening, noticing, and acknowledging where you are in the moment are the first real steps to moving forward. Allow yourself to step with ease.

Bring your attention to your hands and gradually open the fingers of one hand from whatever position it happens to be in at the moment. I suggest working with one hand at a time for ease in focusing your attention. Take your time. Concentrate on opening your fingers in micromovements. The movement is slow, barely discernible to the eye. It can take several minutes to fully open your hand. You might try closing your eyes while continuing to open your fingers.

Although you are working with one hand, you will experience your shoulders settling into a relaxed position. Simultaneous relaxation in your other hand will occur. Your entire body will feel the benefits. Your breathing will become more relaxed, and you might find yourself sighing during the exercise. Continue opening your fingers until you feel a stretch. Keep your fingers extended until you find yourself sighing, breathing in deeply, and exhaling. This is not an intentional sigh but one that occurs naturally and spontaneously. Your fingers will resume a relaxed position as you continue the microtonal movement with your other hand. Patterns of movement will be altered slightly by this practice, slowly increasing extension until another level of movement becomes comfortable.

To align the energy along your spine, become aware of the position of your head. Then moving slowly, almost imperceptibly, begin a vertical alignment of your head with your neck. If you were looking down, move your head upward until it feels level and balanced. Follow this with a microrotation of your head from left or right until you are facing forward. After a short while, your shoulders will relax and adjust. This is a rejuvenating experience. You will notice that even the slightest movement will bring your body into alignment along your spinal column. Posture and comfort are automatically adjusted. It takes focus to continue the micromovements. It also develops patience.

You will come to understand the importance of movement, no matter how small. Change and transformation occur in the smallest space. Micromovements bring these transformational processes to attention. The body remembers. Movement can enliven cellular memory in the body. Just as the voice reflects the emotional content of memories, movement stirs body consciousness to the surface. The quality of the movement is what holds the value, for it is the quality of movement that captures the attention. Every movement, no mater how minuscule, is important and worthy of attention. A shift in one grain of sand can move the sand dune.

Microtonal practices encourage exploration of the smallest movements, physically and vocally. Microtonal movement can tune the body and bring bodymind into alignment as does the microtonal voice. As relaxation occurs, alignment is spontaneous. The intention is to play with movement, to abandon expectations, and to truly explore your responses to microtonal processes. Microtonal movement brings attention to subtle, internal shifts because the mind is relaxed, alert, and quick to perceive a new point of balance coming into being. Alignment becomes observable as it is occurring. The bodymind knows what to do to restore balance and alignment.

As body consciousness is stirred, tones and microtones, or sound in some vocal form, might rise up. Vocal meditation practices often compel physical movement. And once you begin a movement practice, it is not unusual for vocal sounding to surface. Go with the microtonal flow. It will take you where you need to be to experience well-being.

4

WEAVING
VOCAL TAPESTRIES

OVERTONE
CHANTING

Overtone chanting is a vocal practice in which overtones are consciously produced at an audible frequency. Overtones are the harmonics that arise in a series of mathematical ratios from the sounding of a single tone. The first overtone vibrates twice as fast as the first tone, or fundamental. The next overtone vibrates three times as fast as the fundamental. Overtones continue up the scale, proportionately increasing in vibratory rate to the first note, and extend beyond our hearing range. They are multidimensional in nature and are equated with cosmic tones, the music of the spheres of which the ancients speak.

Harmonic overtones are contained in vowel sounds whether they are spoken or sung. To create the melodic flute-like overtones in chanting, vowel sounds are produced in the vocal cavity simultaneously with the sounding of one note. A common tendency in the learning stages of overtone chanting is to tense the jaw, neck, and facial muscles. During overtone chanting instruction of groups and individual students, I ask people to be mindful of tension. It is helpful to stop chanting for a moment when tension is experienced and to relax the neck and facial muscles before resuming chanting. Sounding an easy hum restores a relaxed state as do smiling and sighing. Relaxing the body, especially the neck and facial muscles, allows the overtones to ride on the breath naturally without straining.

Harmonic overtones produced in overtone chanting can sound like a symphony of flutes floating in the air. They are nonlocalized with a translucent quality, making their source unidentifiable as they flutter and spiral around the room. The multidimensional, translucent quality of overtones can evoke a transcendent state while chanting. Those new to the practice often do not hear the harmonics, but over time, the subtle sounds become audible. In learning to hear the higher harmonic frequencies of overtones, it is theorized that listening patterns are restructured. The higher frequencies of overtones are said to charge the cortex of the brain (Tomatis 1991) thereby stimulating the release of endorphins, increasing energy, as well as the ability to focus and concentrate.

Overtone chanting and the harmonics of overtones has been explored in a musical and spiritual context by sound healers (Goldman 1992; Purce 1995; Gardner 1997). Generalizations of physiological benefits are postulated as well as the meditative and spiritual qualities of the practice. Overtone chanting is generally said to be uplifting and relaxing for the chanter. However, no in-depth study of experiential responses to overtone chanting over a period of time has come to my notice. There is little information to draw on with regard to either how overtone chanting might be applied in a therapeutic setting or what physical, mental, emotional, and spiritual responses might be generated and under what conditions.

To begin building a database with regard to the application of vocal healing practices, I conducted a small study for my dissertation on responses to overtone chanting and microtonal singing. Responses to my study indicated that sound and breath work together in vocal healing practices and are experienced to different degrees by each person.

In summary, the responses from the overtone chanting group reveal that the practice adds fullness to the voice and opens the way to participate more freely in other forms of vocal expression when the opportunities arise. It is an effective form of meditation, contributes to achieving mental focus, evokes a state of emotional calm, and has the potential to restore physical health. One person in the group reported the remission of glandular swelling in her throat, a condition that had persisted over a period of months prior to beginning the overtone chanting practice. The practice of overtone chanting can reveal joyful exuberance as well as uncover sorrowful emotions and anger. It was also found to elicit agitation and irritability rather than peace and calm. Deep-seated emotions that surfaced not only awakened awareness and insight but served as a guide in acknowledging and embracing those aspects of the self that needed to be healed.

The insights of the overtone chanting group related primarily to relationships and life goals. Responses ranged from interacting with others more positively (for example, resolving long-standing issues with people) to reaching a point of clarity about life direction and changing a course of study. Awareness of having constructed a worldview around accommodating others ultimately allowed one person in the study to attain what she described as mental freedom. This was coupled with feeling grounded and secure. Overtone chanting appears to be transformative at an emotional, psychological level that ultimately allows the spirit to shine.

Overtone chanting while driving was reported by all participants to be relaxing and easier. They felt secure to vocalize in their cars, unheard by others. The car and the shower are wonderful places to hear overtones because they are reflected back from the windshield and the shower walls. However, some practitioners caution their students not to chant while driving a car or while in the shower because of the transcendent state that can accompany the practice. For this reason, it is always wise to pay attention to the effect of vocal practices on your state of consciousness, especially in the car. If it does not feel safe to sing or chant, don't.

HUMMING

Humming is frequently initiated unconsciously. It has been my experience that some people are not even aware that they are humming unless it is brought to their attention. Humming typically emerges as a melodic tune in a soothing natural voice. The tune is not necessarily a particular song melody but is often of a repetitive nature.

The hum, like a drone, has a grounding effect. It stabilizes. Humming serves to anchor or ground the spirit while creating a sense of harmony. The hum provides a constant point of reference to the Self. It becomes the background against which the melody of living can play and create.

Humming for health involves the production of a non-melodic and continuous humming tone. Begin to hum by vibrating low from the center of your chest, from your sternum. Pay attention to the experience of your humming voice. You will begin to notice that humming soothes your being by giving the body a sonic massage. Continue humming for at least ten minutes, preferably longer. As you become more deeply engaged in your humming process, waves of sound emanating from you will become apparent. Notice the vibrational waves expanding outward as rings in water when a pebble is tossed into a pond. Another transcendent response to vibrational waves of the humming voice is that of joining with pure consciousness while experiencing a sensation of the physical body falling away.

Humming calls attention to the vibrational quality of the voice. Humming in a group expands vibrational awareness within the group and unifies the energy field. Follow your instinct to stop and listen periodically when you are humming with one or more people. Whether humming alone or with others, remain in the silence for a few moments when you finish humming.

Breath is the creative source of Spirit. In humming, speaking, and singing, Spirit flows on the breath and is given living form. Just as you are the humming presence in the silence, you are the creator of inner calm. Sometimes tunes play through our minds evoking spontaneous humming or singing. At those times, just hum softly, the way people do to comfort a child. The child you are comforting is the one living within, the child you carry in your heart who is you.

SACRED SOUNDS

One cannot study sound as healing without looking at belief systems that rely on the power of word in the form of prayer, song, and incantation to invoke healing and transformation from the spiritual or invisible realm. Seeds of ancestral wisdom with regard to the voice reside within healing practices of cultures around the world. Vocal sound healers in the United States are discovering those seeds of ancestral wisdom rising up from within. The need to tone vowel sounds or hum or sing in a universal language of vocables spontaneously presents itself. At this point in time, there is no blueprint to follow. If the ancients are said to have healed a person by sounding one note on a lyre, we are not made aware of the ailment that needed healing or the specific tone that was played. We live in a time of rediscovery as we map the healing properties of tones, not just musical tones played on an instrument but vocal soundings as well.

The sacred sounds of vowels, mantras, and vocables are the healing vessels of the voice.

TONING
VOWELS

Toning, sometimes called sounding, is most commonly defined among sound healers as the sounding of a sustained single note using a vowel. Toning sounds can be produced using a vowel or a combination of consonant and vowel; it is not possible to sound a tone using only a consonant. Vowels have a vibrational quality as they flow on the breath and give sound to the consonants.

Vowels are the most sacred of sounds in many ancient traditions (Abram 1996; Black Elk and Lyon 1990). Ritual practices in which vocables are spoken, chanted, or sung call on primordial awareness of the power of vowels to create and transform. It is the unique vibrational qualities of vowels that create form. Because these sacred sounds of creation are found inside us and can be brought to conscious awareness through vocalizations, the human voice is regarded as an instrument of regeneration and transformation to be used with reverence. When chanted, toned, or spoken in prayer with specific purpose and intent, vowels bring transformation at every level of being (Gardner-Gordon 1993; Keyes 1990).

Vowels are basic primordial sounds insofar as they hold the vibrational energy of life. They live in the elements. They live in the earth. Primordial sound is the creative force of the universe. When we allow our voices to rise up from the earth, we call forth primordial tones. Primordial sound flows through our voices and rides on the pulsing life force of breath to connect our physical bodies to Spirit. It is the vibrational, creative quality of vowels that resonates in our bodies and resounds in the air around us when we call them forth through toning, song, chant, vocable and mantra sounding, and spoken words.

Vowel sounds are associated with the seven major chakras. There is no agreement among vocal sound healers, however, regarding the application of specific vowels to specific chakras. I generally tell people to sound the vowel that feels right for them. For example, I place the "oh" at the first, or root chakra, because it is produced farther back in the throat than "ooo" (as in moon) (Jannedy, Poletto, and Weldon 1994; Feld 1994). The Kaluli of New Guinea also attribute a downward direction to the "oh" sound (Feld 1994). Among the Mikmaq, a Cheyenne culture, "o" indicates the animate force (Alford and Henderson 1992). The animate force can be related to the Kundalini energy of spiritual awakening, which resides in the root, or first chakra. The physical body is identified with the first chakra. The vowels, colors, and musical notes that I associate with specific chakras are as follows:

Chakra	Vowel Sounds	Colors	Notes
1st (Root)	Oh	Red	C
2nd (Sacral)	Ooo	Orange	D
3rd (Solar Plexus)	Aw	Yellow	E
4th (Heart)	Ah	Green	F
5th (Throat)	Eh	Blue	G
6th (Third Eye)	Ih	Indigo	A
7th (Crown)	Eee	Violet	B

Toning is an essential practice in microtonal healing. It flows naturally from microtonal singing, and it can also stand alone as a practice to stabilize and soothe, to clear the energy field, and to balance chakras. Toning specific vowels with an intention to clear the chakras will restore balance and harmonic resonance. The resonant qualities of toning vowels can be experienced within the body. Each vowel will affect different parts of the body and sometimes be felt as a contraction-like sensation. As indicated in the chart above, you can also sing specific notes and visualize corresponding colors to clear and balance chakras.

Toning begins from a place of grounding and is best performed while standing and drawing energy upward from the earth. Your seed tone, that center of soul essence that sustains you, rises up through you. You will know when you have sounded your seed tone. You will feel grounded, aware, alive, and conscious on many levels simultaneously. My use of the term "level" is not to imply a hierarchy. Rather, I imagine layers of being that constantly shift in and out of conscious awareness or focus. There is always a simultaneous unconscious awareness of your internal, external, mental, physical, emotional, and spiritual levels of being, but it is seldom that a person is consciously aware of more than one level or aspect of being in any given moment. Toning can facilitate multilevel and multidimensional awareness.

Toning tends to transport consciousness and invites a meditative state. The tones that emerge can take on the quality of singing bowls, round and full, inviting you to step into the sound of the single note you are toning. It is almost impossible to produce a clear and unwavering vocal tone without focusing on the sound, entering it, and feeling its pureness.

There is a clearing of energy in the space of the tone that is felt and appreciated physically, mentally, emotionally, and spiritually. A wonderful aspect of experiencing the rich quality of a single tone is realizing that pure tone lives within each and every person, just as surely as the silent space dwells within. It is from that silence that the tone arises.

Toning is a natural vocal spiritual practice. It frees the mind because of its nonverbal quality. Sound one tone for twenty to thirty minutes. Listen with the expanded awareness of your whole being and experience the fullness of the note as if it were radiantly aglow with feeling. At one time, this is how people listened to music. A listener plunged into the notes for the purpose of uniting with the Source (Tame 1984). Experience different tones in this manner and notice the qualities and effects of each note in every aspect of your being. As with other toning techniques discussed above, you can do this practice with different notes and vowel sounds to tune each chakra. Notice your responses to different toning techniques until you develop the ability to distinguish the wellness benefits of each method.

Trace the motion of breath in your voice. As swirling eddies of sound are filling your voice, making it rich in texture, acknowledge the beautiful integrity of your voice, so full of the life force. Be *in* your voice. Enter its fullness, its resonance. Play in your voice. Work at coming to know your voice with all of your senses. Feel your voice physically, mentally, emotionally, and spiritually. Vocal healing practices are psychically full. They access and express the soul of emotion. Listen deeply to your voice. Notice its distinct tonal qualities and characteristics. See your voice as beautiful ribbons of colored light or as shimmering sunlight on a clear and flowing stream. Then notice the flow of your voice, smooth in places, rippling in others. Explore the intricacies of your voice. In this way, you will come to understand and know every strand of emotional energy and be able to direct it along its healing path.

When you are toning vowels, pay attention to whether some are more easy or difficult to sing. Notice if you consistently omit particular vowels during your practice of toning or overtone chanting. For example, one client left out "oh" and was not sure why. When I told her that "oh" is associated with the root chakra, she said, "Oh, the one I'm ignoring in my life. That's probably significant." It is significant. The area of life that needs attention and balancing can become apparent through omission. Spend a few minutes each day toning vowels to clear and rejuvenate the chakras.

MANTRAS

A mantra is a sacred Sanskrit word that is used as a focus of meditation. A mantra is food for the soul. Its essence is sound, and it carries vibrational energy even when silently repeated as in Transcendental Meditation. The meaning of a mantra does not need to be understood for the practitioner to experience positive effects. The physical benefits said to result from chanting a mantra or sound repeatedly include decreased heart rate (by approximately three beats per minute), decreased muscle tension, increased alpha (8-13 Hz.) and theta (4-7 Hz.) brain waves, and lower blood pressure, pulse, and rate of metabolism (Achterberg 1985;

Goldman 1992; Ostrander, Schroeder, and Ostrander 1979).

The creative power of sounding mantras with elongated vowel sounds was demonstrated by Hans Jenny (1974, 1986). Jenny experimented with cymatics, a study of the effects of vibrations and tones on substances such as powder, liquid, and metal filings. He laid the foundation for understanding the effect of vibrational frequencies on matter by observing that each vowel, like a mantra, has a unique vibrational structure that manifests itself in a specific form. Each mantra, for example, produces a specific geometric, mandala-like shape. When a mantra is sung, it causes a pile of dust to form precise geometric shapes. Tones of different frequencies produce individual patterns, sometimes resembling snowflakes. Mantras have the power to form structure. They can be used to restore coherency within the energy field, thereby initiating alignment and balance at a physical level.

VOCABLES

The most sacred sounds have no lexical context. The more meaning that is present in speech the more possibility there is for distortion. Vocables, sometimes referred to as nonsense syllables, nonwords, or obsolete language (Frisbie 1980; Halpern 1976), can be considered patterns of primordial sounds rather than words. They carry emotional intent that is beyond words.

Because vocables are spontaneously emerging among sound healers in the United States, the description of vocable use among cultures studied by ethnomusicologists (Briggs 1996; Frisbie 1980; Katz 1982; Halpern 1976) has caught my attention. I draw no conclusions from the observations presented here with regard to the role of vocables in healing. I simply take note of possible similarities and differences in how vocables are perceived and used by sound healers in the United States and among the following referenced cultures.

Although vocables occur almost everywhere, according to Eliade (1974), and are used to communicate with spirits, I was not aware that the application of vocables varied among cultures. According to ethnomusicologist Ida Halpern (1976), vocables are fixed in the music of the Pacific Northwest Coast Indians. Charlotte Frisbie (1980) also reports the use of fixed vocables among the Navaho. It is my understanding that fixed vocables do not change and they are repetitive. On the other hand, Katz (1982) tells us that among the Kalahari !Kung, the vocable syllables change from one singing to the next. They are not fixed, although the songs are the same.

Briggs (1996), who discusses vocables among the Warao in Venezuela, does not mention whether they are fixed syllables or not. He does indicate that vocables are not intended for human communication. They are sounds received from spirits by healers performing curing ceremonies.

Among sound healers I have observed in the United States, vocables arise spontaneously and are not fixed because they change from one singing or chanting to the next. There is no set of established vocables that is said to be applicable to a particular illness or situation. There are some

117

vowel sounds associated with different areas of the body, as indicated earlier, but those associations do not appear to be present in vocable soundings. The vocables can be repeated a few times somewhat rhythmically once they come forth.

Vocables are sometimes thought to be from Universal Mind and thus constitute a language not of this earth but of the invisible realm. Vocables received from the invisible realm are believed to convey the healing power of Spirit. The sound healer is thus the vehicle and not the source of the healing energy being transmitted through vocable soundings.

Another way sound healers in the United States use vocables is to express emotions. Joy Gardner-Gordon (1993) refers to vocables as "gibberish," and in addition to using the nonlanguage as a vehicle of emotional expression, she suggests that it loosens up the voice in preparation for toning.

Vocables draw attention to their sounds rather than to meaning. It is the sounds that hold information and facilitate the way for release and healing. Words can be ignored, but we must pay attention to sounds, to subtleties and inflections, to the roundness and fullness of tone, or to the crispness of slender sounds that cannot escape notice. In listening to the sounds, it becomes easy to catch the space between where emotion lives. With vocables, we are concerned with eliciting emotional expression. Sometimes one syllabic sound says it all.

With vocable expression, you have no idea what syllabic sounds are going to come out. They cannot be rehearsed. They spring from the moment. The same is true with microtonal exploration. You are finding your way, which is how most of us live our lives. Sometimes vocables are repeated one or more times. I can't tell you if this occurs because the sound is pleasing or if it is the sound itself that is speaking for an emotion that wants to be heard. Vocables could be releasing an emotional charge that has been held silent for so long that it bears repeating. And again, there is no true repetition. It is likely that the strength or emphasis or softness of the same syllables will shift as they continue to flow in succession. Sometimes they build in intensity until a tonal hum emerges to restore balance—a reminder that the emotional event is past. The hum emerges as if to say, "This is now and you are safe."

Vocables live in the moment. For example, I have voiced "Ogirrepah ponatiti. Shula ri emmm." These sounds most likely will not surface again in the exact sequence or hold the same emotional content that they express for me right now. As I repeat these sounds now on the printed page, they touch something in my heart, and I can only experience the sensation. It is as if they summon an emotional space for me. Pausing between the two phrases is necessary. It is a healing space. It seems as if the first sequence of vocable sounds holds an emotional pain. The last phrase comforts and reassures. In the pausing space, something shifts and reassurance follows. A verbal analysis of vocables is not part of the healing process. Vocables are to be experienced at a visceral and emotional level and not analyzed.

It is possible that vocable utterances constitute words in some language. For the speaker, however, there is only emotional content in the sound of nonverbal syllabic phrases. Vocables fully and completely honor emotions as nonverbal experiences. Vocable phrasing is free flowing and can continue indefinitely. It can also constitute only one syllabic sound that may or may not be repeated.

Sometimes words get in the way because they flow from the logical mind in an attempt to justify our experiences or to make sense of them by providing order and meaning. Vocables bypass the logical mind. They allow us to directly access the emotional content of our experiences while detaching from meaning. It is as if you listen to your story with a compassionate ear. You can also be led to a place of amusement and humor at hearing these nonsensical sounds rolling off the tongue.

In becoming familiar with your own sounds, you are coming to know the emotional expressions of your own stories. It is less personal because the language with which the stories are expressed is meaningless to the conscious, linguistic mind. The sounds emerge from a soul level within the cells. They are not preconceived at a cognitive level. The sounds are unintentional in that a vocable chant or syllabic sounding might come to mind, but what is spoken or sung is entirely different from that which was consciously intended. With such an occurrence, it becomes apparent that the sounds are not consciously contrived but flow either from a place of inner knowing or are received from a higher consciousness through the space between worlds.

INTEGRATING VOCAL
HEALING PRACTICES

Many travel the road to awakening the healing voice, and for each traveler, the journey has a unique landscape. Ultimately, each person is their own tour guide because the stories and textures that shape a person's life are distinctly personal as are the sounds that will activate healing processes. Having an array of vocal techniques available and understanding the characteristic responses to specific vocal practices is essential to using them for optimum benefit. This section offers some guidelines as to which practices most directly access emotions, which practices soothe and relieve emotional buildup, and which practices provide a means of achieving focus, grounding, and a transcendent state.

Microtonal healing involves an integration of vocal practices. Microtonal singing embodies that integration more than any other vocal healing practice. The vocalizations inherent in microtonal singing work naturally to restore balance. It is also a practice in which the voice is actively and intuitively working with the emotions. For these reasons, more resolution is built into microtonal singing. There is a point when balance is naturally restored.

Microtonal singing and overtone chanting can work together in a complementary fashion. The reasons for combining them become apparent upon deeper examination of their characteristics and beneficial qualities.

Microtonal singing is a process in which the practitioner directly experiences working with the emotions. Vocal fluttering and wavering initiates the process by loosening the emotions and calling them to the surface. The quavering and sliding microtonal voice then modulates emotional energy into a place of balance. Any rough emotional edges are smoothed in this process. Alignment is secured with a steady tone when the voice connects with a svara. Sliding from one note to another can also bring a sense of momentary anticipation followed by release when the voice reaches its destination and settles into pure tone.

In contrast to microtonal singing, overtone chanting does not serve as a channel of emotional expression nor does it accommodate emotional release during the practice sessions. The practice places one in an experience of producing a steady and powerful sound that supports the delicate harmonics of overtones as they ride on the breath. Awareness is more external and transcendent because the focus is on listening to the overtones. Even though the deep breathing involved in the practice of overtone chanting can access emotions from the depths of one's being, emotional activity appears to be delayed. Emotions tend to surface after a chanting session in the course of daily life. Observation of interactions in social situations is likely to occur from a somewhat detached stance. This tends to be followed by insightful awareness of self in relation to others that can be accompanied by resolution. Clarity with regard to life goals also occurs with overtone chanting, sometimes prompting a career change or a shift in priorities.

An attribute of overtone chanting is that it prepares the way to give attention to aspects of emotional life that require healing. Attentiveness in listening to overtones while chanting stimulates mental focus. Mental focus can contribute to a stable sense of self. The steady tone sounded in overtone chanting is not that produced in toning. Rather, it is lower and sometimes more nasal, which generates a sense of body consciousness that is also grounding. In addition, the higher frequencies of overtones can create a hypnotic state and generate an inner calm. These are the conditions that ready a person to handle emotions that might arise. When we are relaxed, focused, and grounded in who we are, it is safe for emotions to surface. The presence of focused stability and calmness summon the inner strength to deal with even painful emotions when they arise in daily life.

When the depth of emotional suppression is severe, the intensity of emotions that lie in unconscious harbor can bring surprise, amazement, and can even stun a person with their unexpected arousal. Emotions can be raw and open when they surface, and insights do not necessarily accompany them. It is worth noting that people are often moved to integrate melodic singing with overtone chanting. Adding melody to the practice is helpful in soothing emotional tensions that arise. Almost immediately, a sense of joy is instilled by the singing; with it, come insights. It is not uncommon for this to be followed by an awareness, a sometimes tearful awareness, with regard to life patterns and self in relation to others. Intuition is awakened with vocal healing practices, which undoubtedly accounts for melodic singing that spontaneously arises from overtone chanting. Following your intuitive knowing naturally guides you to a practice that heals and restores well-being.

There is an awareness of emotionality in vocally producing microtones, and microtonal singing provides a method of working with the emotions, whether the content is conscious or not. Fluttering and wavering into pure tone is an important part of the healing process in microtonal singing. It brings resolution in some instances and can open the way to go deeper at other times. Potential for healing is inherent in the practice. By purging emotions through microtonal expression and by singing the rough edges microtonally, emotions are smoothed into balance and alignment with pure tones or a microtonal slide. Insights emerge from the practice that relate to life processes, and issues are resolved in that context. There are times, however, when it feels appropriate and even necessary to move into sounding overtones.

Overtones do not seem to be as tangibly connected to the body as do microtones because microtones are experienced as direct sounds of the physical voice. Although overtones arise from the production of vowels in the vocal cavity, there is a sense of disconnection from them because of their nonlocalized nature. Overtones resemble flute music that appears to come from somewhere in the distance. It is difficult to identify yourself as the source of overtones when they are heard floating in the air.

Intervals of silence are an important aspect of microtonal singing because they allow stable tones or microtones to stand alone between the silence. Sound supported by silence settles the mind into attentive focus. Rather than remaining caught up in the activation of emotions, moments of silence offer a space for being reflective or empty, or simply being. The place of silence can bring a sense of completion, and it might feel appropriate to end the practice session. Because the practice of microtonal singing engages the emotions, it can be difficult to consistently sustain the practice over a twenty-minute period. Most people feel complete after five or ten minutes. By contrast, overtone chanting can be sustained easily for as long as an hour.

Punctuating overtone chanting with periods of silence deepens its attributes of mental focus and inner calm. The length of the silent space determines the depth of the experience.

Overtone chanting is a practice that displays the voice in a solid tone enhanced by overtones. It strengthens the voice thereby enhancing personal image and presence, because when we are heard, we are seen and presence is acknowledged. The ability to express is also awakened in overtone chanting. It motivates people to act and to speak up for themselves, whereas previously they may have been silent or not made waves. This is especially noticeable in those new to the practice. Mental focus and an enhanced sense of self and personal power are often reported.

Perhaps it would be safe to say that while we cannot sustain an emotional space over an extended period of time, an unemotional, even serious space eventually has to recede in favor of emotional lightness. This is the microtonal flow of life. Overtone chanting opens the way for vocal exploration in the form of howling, imitating sounds such as a bell or a chime, and producing a variety of animal and bird sounds from nature. As mentioned earlier, some people are naturally led to combine overtone chanting with melodic forms of singing. Incorporating overtone chanting while singing along with country western music is another way to lighten the mood. With any vocal healing practice, follow where your voice leads you. You will be happy you did. Then notice your intuitive processes spilling over into other areas of your life. Vocal healing practices initiate a process of coming to trust who you are deep within.

Humming one note or sounding a single tone, whether in the form of toning or overtone chanting, stabilizes the emotions. It is not possible to sustain a solid tone from an emotional place. These practices have a grounding and stabilizing effect. If you feel yourself experiencing emotional discomfort or being emotionally carried away from singing or from some forms of vocable expression, returning to a hum or vocalizing a steady tone is suggested. You regain a solid footing from which you can continue with your process when you feel ready.

The voice is a tool with which to sculpt the contours of your emotional body, and each practice has its role in the healing process. Knowing which practices to apply brings the ability to restore and maintain balance and resonance, and to stabilize and ground within easy reach. Attentiveness to your responses to different vocal practices will reveal the tonal medicine that is most beneficial for you at any particular time. You will come to honor that your vocalizations are unique for each healing.

Keeping a journal of your experiences during and after engaging in a vocal healing practice helps in establishing a record of your healing process. Your journal is a place for reflection, insights, and responses to vocal practices in terms of mental, physical, emotional, and spiritual well-being.

THE TRANSCENDENT
VOICE

Vocal healing practices have a meditative quality. They serve to clear the mind, provide a sense of grounding, center your focus, and instill inner calm. It is the security of being grounded that permits a transcendent and meditative state. A person needs to be anchored to transcend. Being grounded functions as a lifeline and provides a path for the flow of energy.

Physiological changes while singing such as heat rising in the body or overall physical warmth, watering eyes, or fluttering eyelids signify an altered state of consciousness, an aware trance state, as occurs in hypnosis. These physical changes are indicators that I look for as a clinical hypnotherapist. They typically occur after about ten minutes of singing or being involved in the hypnosis process. Meditative states result from an increase in alpha and theta brainwaves that transport consciousness to higher frequencies of expanded spacetime. Microtonal singing, overtone chanting, toning, and humming are all effective meditation practices. The meditation experience differs by practice, although the differences are subtle.

Overtone chanting is a practice for grounding and transcendence. Sounding a solid tone has a grounding effect as it vibrates within the body. The high frequencies of overtones can produce a transcendent or hypnotic state. The harmonics transport consciousness, bringing awareness to finer dimensions of sound while remaining mindful of the tone from which the harmonics arise. Noticing the breath while overtone chanting cultivates a relaxed state and can develop into a focus meditation practice.

Microtonal singing is a more devotional practice that adds rapture to transcendence. It is a physical, bodily experience especially when singing with nature. There is a direct relationship between the flexible structure inherent in microtones and the flow of life. Because of this, microtonal singing has the distinct attribute of developing into an insight meditation practice that instills awareness of your life patterns and processes. The microtonal voice also evokes creativity, perhaps because surfacing emotions are seeking artistic expression.

Toning and humming are particularly effective in developing vibrational awareness of the environment. These practices reveal a physically tangible dimension of sound both internally and externally. Toning, with its full, rich textures, pulls a person into the sound and gives rise to an expansion of consciousness. Transcendence follows the grounding nature of the tone being drawn up from the earth. The tendency is to enter the sound as it encompasses the bodymind and to experience its resonant qualities from a transcendent state.

Humming a low tone that emanates from the sternum induces a meditative state using vibrations. Rings of sound are felt first in the body. From there, consciousness rides vibrational waves until they merge with the environment. If you are humming with another person or with a group, the vibrational waves evolve into a unified whole. The experience is one of existing within vibrational, transcendent waves of energy.

Humming and toning awaken body consciousness to the vibrational nature of life. You can allow your hands to listen with outstretched fingers to sense the vibrations in the air around you as you sound. Vibrational awareness begins within the body. Awareness then extends to the vibrational sensations of vocalizing on the outside of your body. Over time, the environmental energy assumes a tangible quality especially with humming.

SOUNDING WITH INTENTION

Singing for the purpose of healing is not a part of our cultural heritage. Singing is entertainment for most people and is considered something outside our own talents. Song is not cultivated in every individual with a voice, yet it is not uncommon for a parent or a caretaker to hum or sing a lullaby to an infant or small child. At those moments, the intent is most often to soothe and calm.

Cook (1997) as well as Peat (1994) indicate that it is the song that heals not the singer. In my mind, it is difficult to separate the song from the singer. Without the voice, the song has no life because the voice fills the song with the emotions of the singer. Where there is loving intention in singing, it is powered by the emotion of the singer. Perhaps this is why emotions and sentiment are integral to the healing ceremonies and rituals of the Temiar (Roseman 1991), the !Kung (Katz 1982), and the Kaluli (Feld 1994, 1996). The emotions carried in the song hold healing potential. Emotions transport the song to the invisible realm of Spirit, and intention

129

directs the healing energy to a specific area of concern.

Singing with intention initiates a conscious process. When the voice accesses the space between with the intention to heal and create positive transformation, it becomes a conscious link to the Source, to Spirit. Singing with loving intention for purposes of healing is a prayerful act. Is it the prayer that heals or the loving intention in offering the prayer? They work hand in hand and cannot be separated.

Sing with intention frequently even for a brief duration. Benefits are not necessarily proportional with the amount of time you sing, tone, or chant with intention. That is the way of energy medicine. It is your prayerful intention while singing that matters. Trust that this is so. In addition to directing the sound of the voice with intention, colors can be mentally and vocally directed to heal or soothe the physical body as well as to clear the energy centers or to restore coherency in the auric field.

The power of intention can be equated with the power of presence. Sense your presence as solid and firmly planted like a tree in the earth as you direct your voice with light and love. Allow the golden light of love to fill your voice as you focus prayerful intention on family, friends, or even on creativity and clarity for yourself. The voice is a multidimensional vehicle. Through the power of loving intention, the healing presence of song and chant is immediately projected to the point where it is needed within the energy field. Time is not a factor in the invisible realm; therefore, no time is involved in transmitting healing energy. Encompass the essence of all living beings with the light of love that flows from your voice and know that healing energy is reflected back to you for your own well-being.

Because the voice is a powerful initiator of healing and transformation, sing with loving intention toward that end. Sing for yourself. Sing for others. Sing for the healing and restoration of balance to the earth. Sing for world peace. Sing with your intentional voice of love, with your intentional voice of Spirit, with your intentional voice of healing and transformation. Let your essence shine with unconditional love of life. Your voice will naturally reflect the radiance within and plant seeds of joyful transformation in the universe. Sing with loving intention and pure tones will flow from you. Speak with loving intention and healing words will flow.

5
FINAL NOTES

AFTERWORD

M icrotonal healing is a process of following the voice of
the heart by allowing the heart to sing its wisdom. It
involves an integration of vocal practices that are naturally
present in microtonal singing. The practice enhances intentional awareness of subtle energetic shifts by noticing the
voice. The free-flowing quality of microtonal singing serves as
a connection with the natural perfection of human folly. It
calls forth compassion for self and others in a diverse and
imperfect world. It takes consciousness to the space between
realms and beyond to experience oneness with Spirit.

Therapeutic process operates on an interplay of conscious and unconscious activity as microtones follow the way
of the Tao. Microtones arise from the mystery and guide emotional energy through the healing space of transformation
between the visible and invisible realms. The voice knows no
boundaries. We can touch all dimensions with the voice.
Follow your microtonal voice and it will guide you with the
wisdom of your body, connect you to the heart of the earth,
and lead you to the light of Spirit.

The voice is vibrational medicine that works directly
with emotional energy. It is this link to emotions that
empowers the voice to create change and initiate healing
transformation. Those new to microtonal healing will benefit

135

from guidance in learning vocal techniques to express, modulate, soothe, and ultimately release emotions that are inhibiting health. Many vocal sound healers have paved the way in using the healing voice for transformation and well-being. This is the gift they offer to others. Finding a sound health educator or facilitator who is grounded in microtonal healing processes will aid you in developing an understanding of how to work with your own healing voice.

Gathering in groups offers a context for continued exploration of the healing voice. They provide a forum for exchanging and sharing people's experiences of and responses to various vocal practices. Group work can deepen the meaning and significance of engaging in vocal sounding for health. Although the meaning is personal because it arises from within each person's story, the epoch experiences of living are often similar to what others discover in the process of singing.

We experience a multitude of microtonal spaces in the course of a lifetime. They are opportunities to examine the world from a new perspective. Singing the spaces along the way fills the soul with vibrance and vitality. It awakens consciousness to the microtonal flow of life. Movement over peaks and valleys and through silent spaces between events is accomplished with greater ease and lightness of step. It becomes possible to flutter on the wind and to ride the current of life with open eyes of the heart. The world becomes fresh and new. All of this imbues the practice of microtonal singing with meaning for those adventurous enough to taste its blessings.

Every moment is a microtonal space in which to explore the center of the universe. At the heart of the universe is love. By nurturing ourselves, we nurture those around us. If each person took five minutes a day to live at the center of the universe in the heart of love by singing the microtonal space, ours would be a healthier world focused on love and peace. Allow your heart to sing its microtonal strands of emotional color and you will weave healing sonic light into the world.

* * *

We are in the midst of a paradigm shift, moving out of a mechanistic worldview into one that is organic and recognizes the flow of life. We are in a process of recovery: We are recovering more natural ways of living in balance. Concepts long held by those in energy medicine are being validated by science. They are concepts that traditional cultures have known and accepted without science. We are beginning to acknowledge that we are multidimensional beings. We are learning to embrace a reality beyond the physical realm by consciously working with energy in the invisible realm.

The process of transformation in this paradigm shift draws on the knowledge of two eras as if they are separate fields of energy linked by the present moment. How can they be combined into a new paradigm for the common good? What happens when two diverse fields merge in a nebulous space between? Jenny (1974) demonstrated a visual image of this process using sound to generate form in water. When two different tones were externally applied to water simultaneously, each tone produced a distinct pattern, one a tetragon and the other a pentagon. When the two tones were combined, a third figure, bilaterally symmetrical, was brought forth.

We find a similar occurrence when auric energy fields are combined. Hunt (1996) observed a merging of energy fields between two people in her study. When the energy fields of two entities melded into one, both were transformed. They changed and became identical but unlike either field prior to merging. The new field became more elaborate. This is how I perceive the new integrative medicine. As disciplines come together in cooperative study, coherent integration will transform them into a unified and distinct field. Transformation integrates expanded experiences into a comprehensive understanding of relational being across disciplines.

As a researcher in the healing arts, I envision a merging of the fields in every sense of the term. We need to initiate multidisciplinary explorations of life-healing processes. This includes all of the natural sciences, social sciences, mathematics, geometry, allopathic medicine, all forms of energy medicine, music, art, and ancient spiritual practices. Each discipline has the potential to contribute a piece to the puzzle. This is the principle of integrative medicine.

We are embarking on a journey of ever-expanding consciousness into a new and all-embracing paradigm. Rooted in three-dimensional reality of time and space with a vision into other dimensions, we can learn to live consciously in the microtonal space between chaos and coherency where a new paradigm is coming into being. We need to bravely step into that space where unity exists. Agreement arises when respect and harmony are in line with natural laws that accommodate diversity in a shifting universe. As science unfolds laws of the universe that embrace the invisible realm of Spirit, we can unite for a common purpose to expand healing and peace from the microtonal space within each person. Such expansion touches multidimensional realms with healing energy. There is no limit to how far our thoughts of loving intention for peace and well-being can extend.

DREAM IMAGE

What is microtonal healing? That is the question I asked myself when I awoke from a dream in which a book entitled Microtonal Healing had been handed to me along with the task of writing it. It felt as if I had accepted the responsibility of fulfilling the assignment when I received the book into my hands. That was January 1997. In the days and weeks that followed, the dream pursued me throughout my waking moments with a relentless, driving force to delve into microtonal healing, whatever that might be.

Rejecting the assignment was not an option. The idea would not let me rest. I had the impression from my dream that *Microtonal Healing* was an important book for me to write. It contained information about how the voice heals, the focus of my research. The task held me spellbound to unravel the mystery, to connect the dots, so to speak, as they came to my attention.

I have ceased wondering how a person such as myself with no musical training, either vocal or instrumental, could feel so compelled to explore the voice as an instrument of healing. I can only say that I was guided by the events of my life. I had been working with energy healing since the mid-1970s. My work took the form of visualizing color and light, and directing it with a flow of love from my heart for purposes of healing. I knew that each color had a unique vibrational frequency; however, I did not make the connection to music or vocal practices until fifteen years later when I began working with expressive arts as a therapeutic tool.

In an effort to comprehend the healing properties of art, I explored three expressive arts modalities: visual art, sand tray therapy, and music therapy. I realized from my past experience in working with energy that colors and shapes, like sound, have vibrational frequencies. Further, where there is vibration there is sound whether or not it is perceived by the physical senses. In the final analysis, sound is the common, tangible thread connecting the arts as modalities of healing. In my studies, I was led back to ancient traditions, which hold that all of life is created by sound. Sound is sacred. Life springs from the One Vibration, the origin of all that is (Tyson 1981).

My quest to understand the healing voice was launched in 1995 after learning the practice of overtone chanting from Jill Purce, a master of the art who lives in England and teaches internationally. For my master's thesis, I investigated overtone chanting from a transpersonal perspective, that is, how overtone chanting affects body, mind, and spirit. My background prepared me to explore sound healing with an awareness of working with human energy centers as well as the energy field. I wanted to understand what is occurring on every level of being in the process of healing with sound. The exploration of sound healing became both a challenge and a blessing.

The challenge involved wading through explanations of sound healing by way of music theory. Literature that explores the voice as an instrument of healing is only beginning to come into being. Thus far, a theory that supports the assertion of the voice as healing is a mixture of music theory and spiritual concepts that embrace the harmonics of music as creator and transformer. I discovered, however, that when musical theories are present in explanations of the healing voice, the properties of the voice that relate to healing tend to become lost. Musical theories open up areas of investigation far beyond the healing voice. As creator, sound does apply to every aspect of life in the universe. Music theory and mathematical proportions relating to harmonic overtones, chemical elements, distance between planets, and laws of the universe appeared to take center stage, while attention to the healing potential of the human voice faded. The challenges became blessings.

The blessings were twofold: First, because the musical theory of harmonic proportions did not adequately explain to me how the voice is an instrument of healing, I was led to search for an explanation of the healing voice that held meaning for me. Second, in the process of exploring the healing voice, I entered the world of vocal sound healers and came to honor the beauty of my own voice.

With the occurrence of my dream, however, my research took an unexpected turn and new meaning began to unfold. The dream image lingered vividly in my mind's eye: a horizontal band of colors, not contiguous like a rainbow but separated with small spaces between the colors. The colors were only the first three of a rainbow: red, orange, and yellow. My dream also left me with the term "spinal implants." Upon awakening, I puzzled over the dream image and its content. The word "microtonal" was foreign to me and was not to be found in my very old dictionary. "Spinal implants" sounded surgical and certainly outside my area of expertise as a social scientist. To put it simply, I did not understand how I could write a book about microtonal healing and spinal implants when I had no idea what they were.

I could to relate to the band of colors from my dream. It remained embedded in my psyche as I continued with my efforts to comprehend the microtonal healing concept. I sketched it in my notebook with colored pencils and studied it. The spaces between the colors assumed a significant focal point as I thought about microtonal healing. I imagined the infinite shades and hues of color that exist between the seven colors of a rainbow: red, orange, yellow, green, blue, indigo, and violet. The point where one color ends and another begins is not clearly defined. How many shades of color fill the space between red and orange? When does red become orange? When does orange become yellow? I interpreted the lines separating the colors in my dream image as microtonal spaces that hold a range of transitional hues from one color to another. Those spaces also hold the rainbow together.

Translating the visual image of a rainbow into a microtonal concept permitted me to better comprehend what was initially an abstract thought. It was a first step, and it felt solid. I then turned my attention to musical notes. When does A become A sharp or B? I came to regard the microtonal space as a point of transition from one note to another. I surmised that microtones are an infinite range of tones inhabiting the space between two notes. The point where one note begins and another ends occurs in a nebulous space between notes.

Taking the concept a step closer to microtonal healing, I made a leap of assumption and conceived the premise that healing energy is held in the space between notes. It seemed to follow from that premise that healing occurs in the space. The task for me then became one of exploring the microtonal space in the context of healing with sound.

On February 4, 1997, about two weeks after my dream, I had the opportunity in one of my anthropology classes to participate in a Native ceremony conducted by Phillip Scott. Of Cherokee ancestry and a practitioner of traditional native medicine from various tribal cultures, Phillip is founder/director of Ancestral Voice—Center for Indigenous Lifeways in Novato, California. This was not my first experience with Native ceremonies, so I thought I knew what to expect. I was wrong. It was the stuff I had read about, which was both sacred and profound for me.

The ceremony began at 8:30 p.m. and continued for one hour. Phillip spoke easily as he placed a small piece of burning sage into an abalone shell in the center of an altar he had prepared. He took his place in the circle at the opposite end of the room from where I sat. After each of us introduced ourselves, Phillip revealed his ceremonial name and translated it into English. (Omitted here out of respect, for protocol, it is used only in ceremony.)

I remember Phillip began singing in Lakota to Great Spirit and Mother Earth, his voice filling the room with what I now can describe as a vibrant microtonal chanting. After that, I don't remember the sequence of events. I lost track of the order in which the ceremony unfolded, as if it all happened at once. My logical mind had to step aside and in doing so I stepped outside of time.

Phillip played the didgeridoo, an Aboriginal instrument made of a termite-hollowed tree limb often four or five feet in length and about two inches in diameter (although length and diameter can vary from this). It is played with circular breath in which breath is blown through the instrument at the same time the player takes in more air. The result is no interruption in sounding. The sound of the didgeridoo is of a surreal, yet earthly vibrational quality that effortlessly transports awareness. The player also mimics the calls and vocalizations of animals of the forest, desert, ocean, and jungle.

That night, Phillip's playing invoked the presence of my power animal into the circle. A power animal reveals itself to a person in dreaming, visions, journeys, and in real life. It is an Ally and teacher that imparts its medicine, its wisdom, and its behaviors to a person. The presence of my power animal was the first jolt to my senses. At another point, I heard the cry of an eagle and felt the wind beneath its wings on my face. When I opened my eyes, Phillip still sat across the room.

Journeying was accomplished by drumming, which indigenous peoples regard as the heartbeat of Mother Earth. Before beginning, we were given specific instructions to prepare a sacred space on our journey in which to encounter our Animal Ally and/or Guardian Spirit, a "two-legged." We could ask for guidance or healing in our lives and give thanks for our blessings. Phillip signaled to prepare for the journey with a series of drumbeats and then the continuous drumming followed. All of the journeying I have done before or after that evening, although deeply felt and real, pale in comparison. This event was more viscerally alive than I ever imagined possible. After constructing my sacred space in the natural landscape that revealed itself to me, my Guardian Spirit appeared. I invited him to join me. I remember basking in his healing presence, as if I were being infused with healing energy, and then I asked for assistance in understanding my dream and in writing the book. We spoke, but I do not remember what was said. I expressed my gratitude for his help and healing presence. It was then time to return to the classroom. The quickening of the drumbeat called us back.

I was grateful that the space was held and we closed in silence. I had no words. To this day, I carry the experience in my bones. The ceremony remains unrecorded for me beyond what is written here. It lives in my heart and unfolds in my daily life. I continue to feel blessed beyond words. Following that evening, insights began to flow and information came to my attention that fed more insights. I began to take notes and to write.

Six months later, I was still trying to unravel the meaning of my dream. Without a musical background, I had no idea that the concept of microtones existed until I met Silvia Nakkach at the Fifth International Sound Colloquium at Sunrise Ranch in Colorado. Silvia is a musician, singer, and teacher who had been studying the classical music of North India with Ali Akbar Khan for almost twenty years. In facilitating a workshop, Silvia had the group sing "Sa" in a steady tone as we sat outdoors beneath a sheltering tree. Then she instructed us to make it microtonal and slid her voice slightly upward to another note. The term "microtonal" was not used again during the workshop session.

Upon returning home to California, I telephoned Silvia who lives and teaches in the San Francisco Bay area. Although I was working on an evolving theory about microtonal healing, I had no idea what the sound of microtones might be. When I asked Silvia what microtones sound like, she sang them for me, her voice fluttering on a note. She stated that many indigenous people around the world use microtones to heal. As I thought about the healing songs and chants of the Lakota, Apach, and Taos Pueblo tribes that I have heard, it became apparent to me that they are filled with microtones. It is that clear, microtonal quavering quality that brings every cell of my being to full attention when I hear American Indian chanting.

Microtones are inherent in the classical music of North India and I subsequently began studying microtonal singing with Silvia in that tradition. She methodically gave me an understanding of musical concepts using the raga scales. At our first session, she used a dulcimer to demonstrate microtones by plucking a string and simultaneously turning the key used to adjust the tuning. A range of notes slid into the air. "Those are microtones," she said. I came to understand that microtones are indeed an infinite range of tones that exist between fixed notes of a scale. She presented the music of North India as a vocal spiritual practice. It soon became a meditative practice that made way for my consciousness to soar. Thus began the voyage of finding my microtonal voice.

The more I sang microtonally the more I wanted to know about applying the practice of microtonal singing for purposes of healing. I was seeking to understand how the voice heals not in theoretical terms but in a way that speaks to the useful application of vocal practices for healing.

From my experience of microtonal singing, a theory of microtonal healing was taking form. I began to see microtonal healing as a process. Microtonal metaphors were present everywhere I turned, adding awareness and a new depth of meaning to my life. I experienced a renewed reverence for life as sacred in all of its diversity. Before long, an awareness of what I call the "microtonal flow of life" became apparent to me. Placing all life experiences in a microtonal context added substance to microtonal healing. The *Microtonal Healing* book was taking on a life of its own.

The idea of spinal implants still hovered in my thoughts. In the course of my study with Silvia, she showed me a new book entitled *Harmonic Experience* (Mathieu 1997). It is an expansive book on music theory. What caught my attention in the book was Mathieu's introduction of the term "spine of fifths," a term that he describes rather than defines. The spine of fifths provides a visual image of a lattice of notes that progresses up a ladder of staves as a series of fifths. An imaginary, slightly diagonal line runs through several staves creating a musical spine, thus providing a visual harmonic diagram. Although the spine of fifths is meant to serve as a visual tool for the musician, it simply helped me to better understand my dream. If I use the spine of fifths as a model, microtones are the implants along a spine of notes. They have nothing to do with surgically implanting anything into the spine of the physical body.

For purposes of understanding my dream, whether microtones are a range of tones between fifths, such as C and G, is not important. They are simply the range of tones between notes. On the other hand, I continue to wonder if microtones can be implanted vibrationally with the voice in spaces between the vertebrae along the spinal column. Theoretically, there are color frequencies and specific notes associated with each vertebra. What effect singing those notes microtonally into the appropriate spaces along the spine would have is a subject for research and a topic for another microtonal healing book. For now, this book is the first part of the manifestation of my dream.

REFERENCES

REFERENCES

Abram, D. 1996. The Spell of the Sensuous: Perception and language in a more-than-human world. New York: Pantheon Books.

Achterberg, J. 1985. Imagery in Healing: Shamanism and modern medicine. Boston: Shambhala Publications.

Alford, D. M., and J.S.Y. Henderson. 1992. Balancing the Flux. Unpublished manuscript.

Andrews, D. H. 1966. The Symphony of Life. Lee's Summit, MO: Unity Books.

Apel, W. 1973. Harvard Dictionary of Music. Cambridge: Harvard University Press.

Beaulieu, J. 1987. Music and Sound in the Healing Arts. Barrytown, NY: Station Hill Press.

Black Elk, W., and W. S. Lyon. 1990. Black Elk: The Sacred Ways of a Lakota. San Francisco: Harper San Francisco.

Briggs, C. L. 1996. The Meaning of Nonsense, the Poetics of Embodiment, and the Production of Power in Warao Healing.

In the Performance of Healing, ed. C. Laderman and M. Roseman, 185-232. New York: Routledge.

Capra, F. 1980. The Tao of Physics. New York: Bantam Books.

Cook, P. M. 1997. Shaman, Jhankri & Nele: Music healers of indigenous cultures. Roslyn, NY: Ellipsis Arts...

Danielou, A. 1995. Music and the Power of Sound: The influence of tuning and interval on consciousness. Rochester, VT: Inner Traditions International.

Diallo, Y., and M. Hall. 1989. The Healing Drum: African wisdom teachings. Rochester, VT: Destiny Books.

Eliade, M. 1974. Shamanism: Archaic techniques of ecstasy. Willard R. Trask, transl. Princeton, NJ: Princeton University Press.

Feld, S. 1994. Sound and Sentiment: Birds, weeping, poetics and song in Kaluli expression. Philadelphia: University of Pennsylvania Press.

—. 1996. Waterfalls of Song: An acoustemology of place resounding in Bosavi, Papua New Guinea. In Senses of Place, ed. S. Feld and K.H. Basso, 91-135. Santa Fe, NM: School of American Research Press.

Frisbie, C. J. 1980. Vocables in Navajo Ceremonial Music. Ethnomusicology 24(3):347-392.

Gardner, K. 1997. Sounding the Inner Landscape. Rockport, MA: Element Books.

Gardner-Gordon, J. 1993. The Healing Voice: Traditional and contemporary toning, chanting and singing. Freedom, CA: The Crossing Press.

Garfield, L. M. 1987. Sound Medicine: Healing with music, voice, and song. Berkeley, CA: Celestial Arts.

Gerber, R. 1988. Vibrational Medicine. Santa Fe, NM: Bear & Company.

Goldman, J. 1992. Healing Sounds: The power of harmonics. Rockport, MA: Shaftesbury, Dorset.

Greene, B. 2000. The Elegant Universe. New York: Vintage Books.

Halpern, I. 1976. On the Interpretation of "Meaningless-non Sensical Syllables" in the Music of the Pacific Northwest Indians. Ethnomusicology 20(2):253-271.

Hill, J. D. 1993. Keepers of the Sacred Chants: The poetics of ritual power in an Amazonian society. Tucson: The University of Arizona Press.

Hills, C. 1979. Nuclear Evolution: Discovery of the rainbow body. Boulder Creek, CA: University of the Trees Press.

Hunt, V. 1996. Infinite Mind. Malibu, CA: Malibu Publishing.

Jannedy, S., R. Poletto, and T. L. Weldon, eds. 1994. Language Files: Materials for an introduction to language and linguistics. Columbus: Ohio State University Press.

Jenny, H. 1974. Cymatics, vol. 2. Basel: Basilius Press.

—. 1986. Cymatics: The Healing Nature of Sound, Part 1 (Video). Epping, NH: MACROmedia.

Katz, R. 1982. Boiling Energy: Community healing among the Kalahari Kung. Cambridge, MA: Harvard University Press.

Keyes, L. E. 1990. Toning: The creative power of the voice. Marina del Rey, CA: DeVorss.

Khan, H. I. 1988. The Music of Life. New Lebanon, NY: Omega Publications.

—. 1996. The Mysticism of Sound and Music: The Sufi teaching of Hazrat Inayat Khan. Boston: Shambhala.

Lawlis, F. 1988. Shamanic Approaches in a Hospital Pain Clinic. In Shaman's Path, ed. G. Doore, 139-149. Boston: Shambhala.

Lentz, D. A. 1961. Tones and Intervals of Hindu Classical Music (Volume New Series No. 24). Lincoln: University of Nebraska.

Leonard, G. 1981. The Silent Pulse: A search for the perfect rhythm that exists in each of us. New York: Bantam Books.

Levi-Strauss, C. 1975. The Raw and the Cooked: Introduction to a science of mythology, vol. 1. J. Weightman and D. Weightman, transl. New York: Harper Colophon Books.

Lynes, B. 1999. The Cancer Cure that Worked: Fifty years of suppression. Queensville, Ontario, Canada: Marcus Books.

Mathieu, W. A. 1997. Harmonic Experience: Tonal harmony from its natural origins to its modern expression. Rochester, VT: Inner Traditions International.

Menon, R. R. 1974. Discovering Indian Music. Bombay: Somaiya Publications.

Newham, P. 1994. The Singing Cure: An introduction to voice movement therapy. Boston: Shambhala.

Nielsen, L. L. 2000. In Search of Healing Voices: An exploration of sound healers and vocal healing practices. Diss., California Institute of Integral Studies.

Ostrander, S., L. Schroeder, and N. Ostrander. 1979. Superlearning. New York: Delacorte Press.

Padus, E. 1986. Your Emotions and Your Health: New dimensions in mind/body healing. Emmaus, PA: Rodale Press.

Peat, F. D. 1994. Lighting the Seventh Fire: The spiritual ways, healing, and science of the Native American. New York: Birch Lane Press.

Pert, C. B. 1999. Molecules of Emotion: Why you feel the way you feel. New York: Touchstone.

Powers, G. 1992. Sacred Language: The nature of supernatural discourse in Lakota. Norman: University of Oklahoma Press.

Purce, J. 1995. The Unbelievable Resonance of Being. The Singer (February/March).

Roseman, M. 1991. Healing Sounds from the Malaysian Rainforest: Temiar music and medicine. Berkeley: University of California Press.

Rudhyar, D. 1982. The Magic of Tone and the Art of Music. Boulder, CO: Shambhala.

Schwarz, J. 1980. Human Energy Systems. New York: E. P. Dutton.

Tagore, S. M. 1874. Hindu Music. Reprinted from the "Hindoo Patriot," 7th September 1874. In Hindu Music from various authors, ed. and compiler S. M.Tagore, 339-387. 1882 (2nd ed.). Calcutta: I. C. Bose, Stanhope Press.

Tame, D. 1984. The Secret Power of Music. Rochester, VT: Destiny Books.

Titon, J. T. ed. 1984. Worlds of Music: An introduction to the music of the world's peoples. New York: Schirmer Books.

Tomatis, A. A. 1991. The Conscious Ear: My life of transformation through listening. S. Lushington, transl. Barrytown, NY: Station Hill Press.

Twitchell, P. 1982. Eckankar: The key to secret worlds. Menlo Park, CA: IWP Publishing.

Tyson, F. 1981. Psychiatric Music Therapy: Origins and development. New York: Creative Arts Rehabilitation Center.

Waters, F. 1977. The Book of the Hopi. New York: Ballantine Books.

Weil, A. 1995. Spontaneous Healing. New York: Knopf.

Witherspoon, G. 1997. Language and Art in the Navajo Universe. Ann Arbor: University of Michigan Press.

Wolf, F. A. 1992. The Eagle's Guest. New York: Touchstone, Simon & Schuster.

Yogananda, P. 1990. Autobiography of a Yogi. Los Angeles: Self Realization Fellowship.

Zdenek, M. 1983. The Right Brain Experience: An intimate program to free the powers of your imagination. New York: McGraw-Hill.

APPENDIX A:
HEALING VOICE
PRACTITIONERS/EDUCATORS

The following practitioners offer an integration of cross cultural vocalizations for health, well-being and meditation.

Silvia Nakkach, MA, MMT
Vox Mundi School
4053 Harlan Street, #202
Emeryville, CA 94608
(510) 595-0819
e-mail: snakkach@cs.com
www.voxmundiproject.com

Linda Nielsen, Ph.D.
Microtonal Healing Arts
P. O. Box 1094
Langlois, OR 97450
(541) 348-2197
e-mail: lnielsen@microtonalhealing.com
www.microtonalhealing.com

Gina Salá
Cross Cultural Vocal Arts and Healing Techniques
(206) 367-2708
e-mail: ginasala@worldnet.att.net
www.ginasala.com

Phillip Scott
Ancestral Voice—Center for Indigenous Lifeways
108D Oliva Court
Novato, CA 94947
(415) 897-7991
e-mail: Ancestor@gte.net
Nielsen/Microtonal Healin

APPENDIX B: SUPPORT YOUR VOICE
SAMPLE LIST OF CDS

Microtonal/Raga Singing

Chandra, Sheila. Weaving My Ancestors Voices. 1993. Real World.

Dagar, Ustad Sayeeduddin. Music from the World—India: The Art of Dagarvani Dhrupad. Buda Musique.

Lhamo, Yungchen. Tibet, Tibet. 1996. Real World.

Nakkach Silvia. Invocation. 2003. Relaxation Company.

Paul, Russill. Shakti Yoga. 2000. Relaxation Company.

Overtone Chanting

Goldman, Jonathan. The Lost Chord. 2000. Etherean Music.

Gyuto Monks. Tibetan Tantric Choir. 1990. Windham Hill.

Perry, Wayne. The Sounds for Self Healing. 1996. Omni-Musikarma.

Purce, Jill. Overtone Chanting Meditations. 1984. Inner Sound. (Cassette Tape).
(Available from: Inner Sound, 20 Willow Road, London, NW3, England)

Vocal Exploration

Flesh & Bone. Skeleton Woman. 1993. Silver Wave Records.

Heines, Danny. What Worlds They Bring. 2001. Vadadisc.

Nielsen, Linda. Spirit of the Healing Voice. 2004. (Companion CD to Microtonal Healing book. Available from Microtonal Healing Arts, P. O. Box 1094, Langlois, OR 97450 and www.microtonalhealing.com)

Tuvan Throat Singers. Deep in the Heart of Tuva. 1996. Ellipsis Arts.
Nielsen/Microtonal Healing

ABOUT THE AUTHOR

Photo: Imagers West

LINDA L. NIELSEN, Ph.D. is a cultural anthropologist and transpersonal psychologist specializing in vocal healing practices. The research, development and application of a microtonal framework with which to approach healing processes are unique to her work. Her Microtonal Healing Program with groups and individuals involves an integration of microtonal singing with other vocal and sound healing practices, intuitive guided imagery, movement and expressive arts. It was during her advanced studies of social and cultural anthropology that she recognized the widespread use of singing and chanting in healing rituals among cultures around the world. Further research led her to find that harmonic theory did not address the healing process initiated by the voice. Thus began her search for a scientific explanation. She now offers seminars and classes on Microtonal Healing and lives in Oregon. For more information, please visit www.microtonalhealing.com.